Born That Way After All

Born That Way
After All

Dr. David J. Nixon
with R. G. Hamm

Dedication

David:

To my wife Chrissy, for her love, prayer, and support.

And to my parents, David and Mary Nixon, for always being true examples of compassion. Thank you for loving people out-loud.

Glenn:

To my wife Wanda, my best friend. Thanks for your love.

And to my mother Kathleen, thanks for teaching me how to love God with all my heart, soul and mind.

Table of Contents

Acknowledgments

The Henson family, for asking the right question at the right time. God used you. Thank you, Jen.

We would like to thank Dave for his love and dedication to our ministry. You challenge us to be better for the Glory of God!

We would like to thank Steve for his loyalty to truth and his love toward us. God bless you!

Thank you, Jon and Joshua, for your diligence in preparing this work.

Thank you, Marie and Nicole, for your careful edits.

We would like to acknowledge the loyal members of First Love Baptist Church for their prayerful support of this ministry. Thank you.

To every "Sam" in every place, God loves you, and for that reason, this work is humbly written.

Most importantly, we thank our Savior for allowing us to share this wonderful life-changing truth with others and for loving "whosoever."

Introduction

Many young people have left our churches and wandered off into the "gay" lifestyle. They abandon their faith or somehow justify their choices by claiming they were born that way. Why would a loving God create them in a way that is contrary to the Scriptures? They are left struggling through the rest of their life, often falling deeper and deeper into a godless lifestyle and further and further away from their faith. Unfortunately, the Christian world has taken two opposite extremes, both which leave the "gay" individual without honest answers. Some have decided that homosexuality is not a sin. They expect Christians that believe it is a sin to accept these individuals' lifestyle rather than help them escape from their behavior. The other extreme is to deem them hopelessly condemned and to release them into the world with no way back.

It was the providence of God that led us to a young man who fit this exact description. He, like so many others that I have met, sought answers from well-meaning family, friends, pastors, counselors and teachers, but ended up more confused with even stronger feelings of guilt and shame. After years of fighting, this young man, with no desire for women, finally fled away into a homosexual lifestyle that alienated his church, his family, his friends, and his faith. After much study of the Scriptures, I was given the opportunity to explain a biblical, life-changing Truth to this young man. This new knowledge of the Scriptures led him out of the gay lifestyle and back to the Lord and to the church. This was done, not by convincing him that he was mistaken about his feelings, but rather that his feelings were misdirected.

Today he is not living a "gay" lifestyle nor is he denying the truth about how he was born. Instead, he has discovered the real truth about himself. If he is not gay, what is he? In *Born That Way After All* you will discover the truth about this young man. This same truth applies to almost every man and woman who professes to be "gay." If they were not meant to be "gay," what are they? This book was written primarily for these people, to help them understand their unique purpose in life.

Perhaps you are a curious reader or maybe you have struggled with these same questions. If this sounds new or strange to you, you are not alone. Most Christians do not understand the significance of this marvelous, life-changing Truth. Now we can all know the biblical truth that can help those who have been deceived into a life of sin and dishonor. Now we can all know the truth about why some people are born different.

The answers have been there all along, but up until now, we did not understand them. Our prayer is that revival can come to individuals, families, churches, our nation, and even to the world as we address one of the most difficult issues of our day. We will not leave these unique and special individuals to fight the battle alone. We will help them to learn of God's plan for their life. In truth, they were *born that way after all.*

Chapter One
BORN THAT WAY

The Beginning

Some men find a ministry; some ministries find the man. Sometimes a ministry comes directly from the hand of God, because the man would never consider it otherwise. It happened like that for me. God chose a ministry that *I never* would have chosen for myself or even considered could be a "real" ministry.

I have been in Christian service for twenty years. For nine of those years, I have been a pastor. Several years ago in a church where I was the pastor, I started playing a little game during our Wednesday evening services. The game was called "Stump the Dummy," and the dummy—you guessed it— was me. The idea was for people to ask Bible questions that were confusing to them. Some people used it to try and stump me, while others asked questions for which they wanted an answer. Either way, it was always in fun and it generated some interesting thoughts. Needless to say, I did not always have the answer, and when I did not, it forced me to go to my Bible to find it.

One particular Wednesday evening in the spring of 2012, someone asked me a question that would be the beginning of an incredible journey for me. They asked, "If being gay is a sin, why do so many young people, even in Christian homes, struggle with whether or not they are gay?" Had that question been asked one week before, my answer would have been quite different. In fact, it would have gone something like this: "If someone thinks they are gay, they may have been molested, abused, or had some form of trauma in life that has left them terribly confused." I probably would have also suggested that the person was more than likely involved in some type of sexual perversion. However, that was not my answer.

Earlier that week, my Bible study had led me to Matthew chapter nineteen, where Jesus taught His disciples about marriage and divorce. I had read this passage dozens, perhaps even hundreds of times, but something stood out to me that I had glossed over every time I had read it before. In fact, it was like I was seeing a portion of this passage for the first time.

> Matthew 19:11-12 – *But he said unto them, All men cannot receive this saying, save they to whom it is given. For there are some **eunuchs**, which were so born from their mother's womb: and there are some **eunuchs**, which were made **eunuchs** of men: and there be **eunuchs**, which have made themselves **eunuchs** for the kingdom of heaven's sake. He that is able to receive it, let him receive it.*

In the midst of discussing marriage and divorce, Jesus spoke of a subject about which I had read, but never heard taught. He spoke of eunuchs. My curiosity (I know now it was the Holy Spirit) led me to begin a study on eunuchs. I knew what eunuchs were, but within minutes, I realized I was seeing something I had never clearly understood.

In the past, I had always assumed that a eunuch was merely a man who had been castrated, but that was not consistent with what I had read in Matthew. I realized that it was not speaking primarily of a man who had been made a eunuch by surgical means, but also one who had been born a eunuch. The Bible clearly states that there are different categories of eunuchs, including those who are born that way, those who are made that way, and those who choose that way. Then I discovered that the *term "eunuch" was often understood as "guardian," or "nurturer," meaning "one who is meant to remain faithfully unmarried" (see Chapter Four: A New Journey).* I jotted that down in the margin of my Bible next to Matthew 19:12 and went on with my study.

The next Wednesday night I was asked: "If being gay is a sin, why do so many young people, even in Christian homes, struggle with whether or not they are gay?" Because of that brief study, my answer was totally different than it would have been one week earlier. Here is basically what I said in response, "Perhaps the reason why many feel they are gay is that they have never realized they were born as eunuchs." I made a few more comments and then moved on to the next question. I was not completely convinced of my own answer. I knew I needed to do more study, but the wheels were in motion.

Not a week had gone by before I received a call from a lady who had attended our church that particular Wednesday night. She was not a member, but happened to visit that night and heard my answer about being born as a eunuch. She said, "Pastor, I was there and heard what you said about some people being born as eunuchs. My grandson has recently decided that he is gay. Would you be willing to sit down with him and talk to him about this decision?"

What could I say, but, "Yes." Now I was going to have to back up what I had said, forcing me to do a more in-depth study of this passage. I could not merely give my speculative opinions to this young man. I needed to know that I was on scriptural grounds. I poured myself into the study to make certain I was ready.

Looking Back

While I like to think of myself as a compassionate man, there was a time when Johnny Nixon was a fundamental, red-blooded, macho, queer-hating, heterosexual male. Do not misunderstand me. I loved people and I wanted everyone to get saved, but I placed a different expectation on gay lost people than I did on others who were unsaved. It was the culture in which I was raised. I do not believe the culture was meant to be one of hatred. Those thoughts were born more out of ignorance.

I remember as a teenager attending a youth conference and hearing a message preached on being a "true" Christian man. The preacher brought a powerful message, and much of what he said was spot on. I remember one particular part of that sermon quite vividly. In it he used incredibly strong language to condemn "gay" men. He called them names and made violent threats. He said that "real men" should banish "homosexuals" to non-existence. He even said that AIDS was a curse sent from God.

Before I knew it, I was so caught up in the moment that I was standing and shouting, "Praise the Lord!" I can hardly believe that was me, because it was totally out of character for me, but it all sounded so good at the moment.

Clearly, this kind of preaching often takes things way too far, and much of what he said was rhetoric and not what he actually believed. In fact, to his credit, the preacher who preached this message apologized publicly a few years later for the hurtful language and the suggestions of violence in his sermon. However, that was pretty much how we all felt about it at the time. We knew homosexuality was wrong and perverted, and not only that, it was unnatural to us. I believe and continue to believe that it is a sin and an abomination to the Lord.

After graduating from high school, I eventually went off into the military and served in the 10th Mountain Division, 2nd Brigade Combat Team (Commandos). During this time, I also went to bible college and studied for the ministry, later becoming a pastor of a church. My position on homosexuality was pretty standard. It was a sin and an abomination to the Lord.

But in my preparation to speak to this lady's grandson, the Scriptures revealed a different approach and understanding to the topic. Very quickly I began seeing it in a totally different light.

A New Ministry

The grandson's name was Sam. Sam had grown up in a good church in the area. He had been taught right from wrong and, of course, he had heard that homosexuality was a sin. He was active in his church and a willing servant. He was never "one of the guys," but there was no reason to suspect that there was anything drastically different about him.

When I agreed to meet with Sam, I agreed on the condition that we first explain the situation to the pastor of the church in which he attended and in which he grew up. Their pastor knew and loved the family, and I did not want to violate my ethics by secretly meeting with his church members.

6

The pastor and I met the night before my meeting with Sam. At first, he was quiet and said little. Later, he told me that he was suspicious before our discussion, because he feared that I was some sort of "new-age" preacher who believed that people were born gay. I can only imagine what must have been going through his mind, because I would have had the same concerns.

At our meeting, I spent about twenty minutes explaining what I had discovered in the Bible. It was then that the pastor interrupted me. I feared perhaps I was not conveying this truth properly. I was concerned that he was going to ask me to leave and cancel the meeting with Sam. Instead, this fine man of God told me that he had never heard anything like this before, and he definitely wanted Sam to meet me. Then he asked if I would consider coming to his church and teaching this to his people. I agreed. When I finished explaining everything to him, he said something profound, "Pastor Nixon, I've studied that chapter many times. I have seen that Scripture many times. I have seen it, but I have never *seen* it."

That good man encouraged my nervous heart that night. What he said would prove to be the number one thing I would hear from other preachers. He also told me that the Holy Spirit had confirmed it to his spirit almost immediately. Later, I understood why I had been so nervous. It was not a fearful nervous, but the kind of nervous you might experience right before the birth of your first child. I knew God was doing something. Now I know He was birthing a ministry.

The Meeting

The night I met with Sam was one of the most awkward meetings of my life, not because he was "gay," but because Sam had no idea why we were meeting. As our meeting drew nearer, I do not think that I have ever studied so hard for an appointment before in my life. I knew that I had to be ready with answers, not my answers, but answers from the Scriptures. I had requested that his mother and grandmother be present when I met with Sam. I knew what I was going to say and his grandmother knew why we were meeting, but Sam was totally in the dark. In fact, his grandmother took me aside when I first arrived and said, "Preacher, Sam does not know what we are doing tonight, so you handle it any way you wish." Yeah... this was definitely going to be awkward.

Sam's pastor had told me some things about Sam the night before. He told me that Sam was a fine young man. In fact, Sam had been a model youth. He was good to his family and was always ready to assist at church. However, he also told me that Sam was often isolated from other kids and was more likely to be around the adult women in church. He suspected that some of the other boys may have teased him, but he had never witnessed it. Sam's temperament did not appear to be troubled. In fact, Sam would be the first to help a younger child if they were hurt while playing. They even allowed Sam to help teach in VBS before he was out of high school because he was so good with the kids.

After Sam went to college and "came out," the family was crushed. The pastor said, however, this *juicy* news did not surprise many people. When church members asked him about the rumors of Sam "leaving the closet," they always made remarks about how they knew something was different about Sam all along.

When the family explained that Sam had told them he was "gay," the pastor suggested that they tell no one and instead just pray for him. In the weeks that followed, the pastor shared a few of his personal thoughts regarding Sam's "closet confession." He was concerned that this would destroy Sam's family. They searched for blame, but could not find any; after all, Sam's siblings were not at all like him. In fact, they had disowned him. The pastor advised the family not to discuss Sam publicly. He secretly wondered about Sam's salvation, but that was difficult considering how well he knew Sam. This young man seemed sincere in his faith in Christ.

The pastor showed good insight and acted like so many others would. Homosexuality can have a deep effect on families and even churches. So his advice was, if Sam were saved, God would eventually discipline him and restore him to the right way of thinking. The pastor also worried that the young people in church who had been close to Sam would compromise their standards out of sympathy for him. To prevent this, the pastor went on the offense and began a series of sermons against homosexuality. What he and most preachers do not understand is that it is not always as easy as telling them it is wrong, especially when they have things going on in their lives that we do not understand and cannot explain.

The results of the sermon series seemed good, but later he realized that it might have ostracized Sam's family unintentionally. Some in church might have seen his sermons as an opportunity to jab Sam's family. However, the discussions that came from the series were mostly good, and most of Sam's family remained faithful to the church.

The pastor agreed to be there for the meeting, and we met in his study. Sam came in, along with his mother and his grandmother. We shook hands and greeted one another. He was a nice young man. I can only imagine how he must have felt with four of us there "ganging up" on him, but he could not have been more gracious. After exchanging a few pleasantries, I decided to go ahead and deal with the elephant in the room, so I said, "Sam, the reason I am here is to talk to you about your sex life." How is that for blunt?

Sam showed a bit of surprise by my candid confession, but he remained composed and respectful. This was the first time I had spoken to an openly "gay" man without being rude, condemning, or condescending. I had a deep compassion for him. I told Sam what I had discovered in my study of Matthew 19, and I explained what the Bible said about eunuchs. I had a peace and calm from the Holy Spirit as we spoke, and the Lord gave me great freedom and clarity as I spoke to him. Now, it was Sam's turn to speak. I wanted to know about him. I listened, not with prejudice, but with great interest as he told me his story.

Sam's Story

The following is what Sam told me that night:

> *I was raised in a good Christian home, and I accepted Christ as my Savior as a young boy. As time went by, I realized that I had no attraction to girls and it bothered me. I had been taught my*

entire life that homosexuality was a sin. I tried to like girls, I did, but it did not work. There was simply no attraction.

One day I decided to ask Sara, a girl I knew, out on a date. I liked Sara very much and was attracted to her as a friend, but I knew that was all the attraction there was, although I desperately wanted there to be more. Sara was a pretty girl with soft, brown eyes and brown hair that seemed to match perfectly. She wore her hair down for the date, although at school she wore it in braids more often than not. Sara was a nice girl, and even though she was not extremely popular at school, she was well liked by most of the students. I liked her personality, and she had a sincere laugh, which I enjoyed.

The date went well. She seemed to have enjoyed herself, but I had a twinge of guilt, because I knew I had no feelings for her. This was more of a test date for me. In fact, it was my first date ever. Even though I enjoyed spending time with her and had a great time, this date was for a specific purpose. I wanted to find out if I had any attraction to her other than as friends.

"I had a great time," Sara said, smiling with genuine enjoyment.

"So did I," I responded. My palms were starting to sweat as I stood on the porch looking at her.

"Thank you for a great evening," Sara said. Then she placed her palms on my chest, rose on her tip-toes, and placed a quick kiss on my lips. She stepped back, and with a final, "Goodnight," she opened the door and went inside the house. It had been the moment for which I had waited for so long. I wanted to see what and how I would feel.

I walked back to my car and drove the eight miles back home in total silence. I thought of Sara, the date, and the goodnight kiss on the porch. Sara was pretty, smart, and fun to be with, and I enjoyed her company as a friend, but tonight was supposed to be different. It was supposed to be a date, not merely two friends

10

hanging out. I needed that goodnight kiss, not because I wanted to kiss her, but because I needed to see how it felt. What would happen? I was hoping something would actually happen, but there were no butterflies. I felt nothing! I was not attracted to pretty Sara. In fact, I had never been physically attracted to any girl.

It was then I knew with certainty that what I feared was true. I was not attracted to girls. I wanted to feel attraction to Sara. I wanted to enjoy that kiss. I wondered what this all meant. I did not want to think about it. I pulled the car over and began to cry.

For Sam, this was the beginning of the struggle. He was a Christian, yet he knew he was not attracted to girls. He tried several times to force himself, but he could not change his feelings. He dated and went to parties, but nothing helped. He contemplated suicide as many young men in this situation do. One day, he finally made an attempt to overdose using over-the-counter drugs. The thought that he was "gay" was more than he could stand. He was lonely and confused. No one understood.

In the fall, Sam went off to college. He had begun to drift away from the Lord in his guilt and shame. Perhaps he thought the Lord did not want him anymore. At college, a friend invited him to go to a bar with him and he agreed to go. After being there for a few minutes, his friend confessed to Sam that he was gay and that he and others had agreed that they thought Sam was gay as well. He told Sam that he was interested in him sexually.

At the time, Sam had never felt any more attraction to men than he had for women, but he was drawn to this guy because he seemed to understand him without ridicule or judgment. In fact, this was the first time Sam had ever felt like someone identified with him. Eventually, he began to believe that he was gay. After some time had passed, he decided that it was time to let everyone know, so Sam "came out" to his friends and family. All of them were disappointed and most shunned him for choosing to live in that lifestyle. Only a cousin, his mother, and his grandmother refused to turn away from him. Sam had made his choice to admit to the life he thought he was born to live.

The Revelation

It was nearing midnight. We had been talking, praying, and reading the Scriptures for nearly four hours. I carefully shared the idea with Sam that maybe he had indeed been born that way, not as a "homosexual," but as a "eunuch." I explained what eunuchs were, and I assured Sam that they were made uniquely by God for a special purpose. I told him that in my study of the subject, I had come to believe that many young men, who thought they must be homosexuals, were actually eunuchs.

I will never forget what happened that night. Sam began to weep. I could see something different in his eyes. He read Matthew 19:12 over and over again, and then he began to shiver. He looked up at me and then turned to his mother and, through his tears, Sam said, "Mom, *I'm not gay.*" His mom and grandmother began to weep. All of us were crying. He said, *"I'm a eunuch. I guess God did make me special."* What an amazing moment it was for all of us.

The joy was soon turned to conviction because Sam asked me a question that would redefine my ministry. With reddened eyes and a trembling voice, Sam asked, "Preacher, why didn't someone show this to me when I was younger? This could have saved me so much regret." At that moment, I knew a ministry had been born by the work of the Holy Spirit. It is amazing to think that someone like me who had so often treated "gays" as outcast and perverts would now commit myself to helping them understand they were indeed **not** born gay, but that maybe they were created "different" and special—as natural eunuchs. I will never forget the joy of that first experience, when I saw Sam come to the realization that he was *born that way after all.*

Chapter Two

I AM NOT GAY

Coming Out

Sam's discovery was a moment in time that I will never forget, but it was one I would soon experience with others as well. What does a person do when they realize they do not fit in anywhere? Imagine the confusion Sam felt when it first became evident to him that he had no sexual interest or attraction to girls. Put yourself in his shoes and in those of thousands of others who come to this realization.

Most of us always knew what we wanted and thus it was not too difficult for us to "fit in." For people like Sam, it is not that simple. It is far too simplistic for us to cast a stone at Sam and say, "Come on man, be normal." However, why should anyone pretend something that is not there? Sam was not committing any sin. The Bible did not say he had to like girls. He was not at first sexually attracted to men. Sam was a good young man who simply had no answers to "who" or "what" he was.

Imagine that day when the young man at college told Sam that he understood him and that Sam was okay. For the first time, Sam felt a sense of belonging. In his heart, he knew he did not ask to be this way nor did he commit some sin that made him this way, and here, in that bar, was someone who had an answer. No, it was not a biblical answer for which he had sought or wanted, but maybe it was "meant to be" for Sam.

Try to imagine that day when he told his family. Feelings of betrayal caused some of them to turn against him. Feelings of guilt arose in his mom and grandmother. No doubt they wondered what they had done wrong to cause Sam to be different. Imagine the horrible guilt Sam felt when he told them what he must have known would break their hearts and cause some to abandon him.

Then comes the moment when it becomes public. Now everyone is asking questions. Was he molested? Is he saved? Did his mother coddle him? Was she overbearing? All of these questions basically revolved around one specific question: Whose fault is this? Every emotion imaginable swirled around Sam: fear, shame, anger, guilt, hurt, and sorrow. Some of these feelings came from within and others from those affected by what he had "discovered" about himself.

It is far too easy for us to treat this situation in a cold and heartless manner. Most of us would fear the thought of being "gay" more than most anything. What we cannot forget, however, is that the one who feared it most was Sam.

We naturally react when a stimulus comes into our lives. Our reaction depends on many factors, but most often by how something affects us personally. People reacted all around Sam. Each reaction was a dagger in his heart. He did not want to hurt these people. He loved his mom and all of his family. He loved his pastor and his church. He cared what they thought of him. He loved God, and he did not want God to be angry at him. Yet, he knew nothing would ever be the same.

Why do some people in this situation consider and even commit suicide? Is it because they do not want to live anymore? Absolutely not! Sam wanted to live. He wanted to be excited about a future. He did not want to die, but the thought of death seemed easier to him than thoughts of dealing with this horrible "affliction" he felt. Many people treat this situation as an affliction, especially if they are a Christian.

Let me make one thing perfectly clear about Sam and most of the others like Sam that I have dealt with in this situation: no one was to blame. Certain factors may lead to certain *behaviors*, but nothing or no one is to blame for their *lack of desire* for the opposite sex. In most cases, their parents did not abuse them or raise them in some failed manner. Blame is not something that should enter this discussion.

14

A Real Man

Sam was a spiritual young man. He wanted to honor God and his mom. He wanted to serve the Lord. According to his pastor, he was a "model youth." He was never in trouble. He was trustworthy. He set out to "be" what he thought he was supposed to be: a "red-blooded male" that liked girls and wanted to get married and have a family. Sam worked at being "normal," but he could not do it.

Another important fact is that Sam, and those like him, do not start out with a sexual desire for the same sex. They start out realizing that they have no attraction to the opposite sex. Sam never considered himself to be gay at first, but the question that he might be gay persisted because he knew no other option. After all, the absence of an attraction to girls can only mean one thing, right? At least, that's what the culture told him.

I recall the first time my daughter asked me what it meant to be a "gay" man. She had to be only six or seven, and explaining it made me nauseous. My answer is common among parents. I simply said, "Gay is when a man does not like girls." Was my answer wrong? Yes, but not intentionally.

Until I met Sam, I had never imagined what a person like him must be experiencing. How could I? I saw them as "queer" and different from me. They were flawed humans and did not deserve to receive my compassion. They needed "preaching to" or perhaps roughed up a bit to make a man out of them. They needed to repent and turn to God and women. It was after I dealt with Sam that everything changed for me. I have been there and seen all the hurt, the shame, the guilt, and the fear that accompanies this situation. My heart breaks for them. They are special and loved by the same God who loves me.

This leads me to another observation about Sam. Many people assume that all men who are like him are effeminate. Nothing could be further from the truth. Sam was not a "sissy," as we used to call them. He was a man. True, he did not fit the typical mold of what our churches and society define as "manhood," but maybe we need to take a closer look at manhood (as we will do in another chapter). Sam was not like all the other guys, yet

15

he was like them in more ways than not. He was sensitive, yet masculine. He was a man.

A Foreign Country

At the center of everything was the fact that Sam knew he did not fit in. He did not fit in with his friends. He did not fit in with his church. He did not fit in with his family. He did not fit in with his own idea of who he was supposed to be. Sam was a misfit.

Imagine going away to a foreign country to live. No one spoke your language, and you did not speak their language. No one looked like you, thought like you, or practiced the same customs as you. One day, someone came up and spoke your language and said they were from your country. Then they said, "I understand how you feel." You would be thrilled! If you had been in your home country, you may have had nothing in common, but in this context, you felt like you had everything in common. Having a companion would make you feel like you "fit in."

That was exactly what happened to Sam when he went to college. No one at home had recognized his dilemma—at least not enough to say anything. Maybe they were suspicious, but most people who say that are playing Monday morning quarterback, because they most likely did not suspect anything. They may have known something was different, and when they discovered that he was "gay," they say there was no surprise. In reality, I highly doubt they could perceive the total truth of the situation. In fact, Sam was *not indentifying as gay*—at least not at that time.

So here was Sam in that "foreign country." There he met a young man who "understood" something about his turmoil. How good that must have felt. If they were back at his home church, the two of them might never have "clicked," but in that lonely place far removed from home, they did.

It would be easy for us to think that the motives of the young man who approached Sam were in some way sinister. I prefer to think that he was probably another Sam, just a bit further down the road. I have discovered that many have accepted the idea that they are gay, but still feel a sense of guilt and shame. Their past and even their own conscience tell them that it

16

is wrong, but they come to the conclusion that this is the lot that life has dealt them. This young man saw a kindred spirit in Sam. He believed that Sam was someone who would "fit in" his world.

Credit Due

There are two people in this story who deserve a lot of credit. Sam's grandmother obviously loved her grandson. There is no question that God led her to that Wednesday evening service. What I admire about her is the fact that she took action. She believed that this was the answer to their problem. She loved Sam enough to schedule the meeting. It is equally obvious that Sam respected her enough to show up to the meeting. He had to know or at least suspect that this was some type of "intervention." My hat is off to this dear lady. Her passion for God and Sam were essential.

Sam's pastor is another individual that I speak of with high regard. Believe me, there are many reasons some men would have refused to allow this meeting to happen. He could have felt threatened that another pastor was possibly going to "help" one of "his" sheep. He also had to feel some doubt as to my legitimacy and to the scriptural purity of what I was going to share. He approached this with a spiritual mind, and he put his flock first. We must have men like this in our pulpits if we are to help the "Sams" and their families who are out there in this world.

Infirmity

I have no illusions. What Sam so readily received will likely be rejected by multitudes of others who are under the bondage of their sin. However, this truth can still make their families free from the shame that Satan is throwing at them. That is important as well.

It is also important that we realize that Sam's feelings were not sinful. If I could preach this to all of those like Sam, I would beg them not to assume that their feelings mean what Satan wants them to believe. The night Sam drove away from his date, he was feeling a sense of guilt for his feelings— or lack thereof. Satan was filling his mind with doubts about who he "really" was and using Sam's own feelings to create those doubts. There is no sin in how Sam felt. Jesus is touched with every feeling of our

17

infirmities (Hebrews 4:15). Was his struggle to try and understand his feelings an infirmity? No doubt, it was.

An infirmity is anything that makes us different or that we bear in us to accomplish God's purpose. Being born blind can be considered an infirmity, but we must also believe that infirmities do not make us less of a special person before God. In fact, we are chosen to bear these infirmities. Sam was uniquely created by God for a purpose. Once we see that purpose, our infirmities become our calling card for God. Before we understand there is a purpose, however, they bring deep feelings of confusion, hurt and fear.

There were two distinct parts to Sam's discovery that night. Both were vital in their importance. All of Sam's fears, shame, guilt, hurt, and even anger at God were reflected in some of the most amazing words I have ever heard spoken in my ministry. Sam looked at his mom and confessed, *"Mom, I am not gay."*

Chapter Three

I AM A EUNUCH

Dilemmas

Have you ever known you had some type of physical ailment, but you did not quite know what it was? Most of us have, at some time or another, known something was not exactly right, but we had no diagnosis as to what it was. What did you do? Perhaps you looked on the internet to find the symptoms. Sometimes that may be a good thing, but often it leads to panic. You start believing that you have some deadly disease, when in reality it's nothing major.

Self-diagnosis can be dangerous because we may use faulty reasoning as the basis of our diagnosis. Guessing is a terrible way to decide what is causing our ailments. Often, we are left with a dilemma because the options we see are all bad. We hope that a doctor will give us an alternative diagnosis that is less severe.

Life is made up of many dilemmas. A dilemma is something for which we are given two or more choices, none of which are perfect, obvious, or ideal. For example, you may be deciding which route to take to a certain destination. One route has road construction while the other has many traffic lights. You are faced with a dilemma, because neither choice is ideal. Then someone tells you of a better route that you did not even know existed. Suddenly, you realize this is the perfect alternative.

The dilemma that Sam faced was one of the worst imaginable. Here was a young man who knew he did not have any attraction to girls. His dilemma was whether to live as a "fake" and pretend he was attracted to females or to declare that he was a homosexual. Neither was palatable to him. He did not want to live a life that was completely untrue, but on the other hand, he knew that homosexuality was wrong. Unfortunately for Sam, he saw no alternative... until that evening we met.

Getting It Right

Try to imagine the first time you ever did something that involved the life of another person. Think of a young doctor performing his first surgery or an airline pilot flying his first flight in command of the airplane. That is how I felt the evening I met with Sam. I knew I had the truth, but this was the first time I would apply this truth to one who was in need. Sam was not some guinea pig on whom I could merely experiment with my theories. He was a broken young man, and his entire family, and even his church, had been affected by his own diagnosis. There were many things I considered as I prepared for that meeting.

One of my greatest concerns was how far Sam had gone into the homosexual life. Was he completely engaged in the practices? Was he now sexually addicted to this new lifestyle? This is one of the concerns we all have in dealing with someone who has "experimented" with certain sins. We face it with people who are involved in drugs, alcohol and other sexual practices as well. Had Sam gone so far that the road back would be treacherous and rocky? This was a major concern of mine.

Another concern was Sam's willingness to accept the truth. I knew that if he accepted the truth, the truth could set him free, but would he be open to it? Much prayer went into this meeting, asking God to prepare Sam for the truth and give him an open heart ready to receive the truth.

My next concerns were in regard to my own preparedness. It was one thing to give my opinion during a question and answer session with a general audience, but it was much different presenting the information to a person already involved in homosexuality. Sam was convinced that he was "gay." I could not throw opinions and theories at him. I had to be equipped, not only with the truth, but with answers to any questions he may have. I prepared with great diligence for my meeting with Sam. I studied everything I could find regarding this truth in the Scriptures, historical testimony, and medical research, knowing that, inevitably, it was the power of God's Word that would have to prevail.

I found supporting evidence for this truth in many realms. There was historical evidence. There was physiological and psychological evidence. There was testimonial evidence. Yet with all these sources to substantiate what I learned, the **only** thing that mattered was what the Scriptures taught on the subject. All the other sources would be useful to help enlighten us in a practical way.

One last concern was what would we do if Sam believed what I showed him was true? Then what? There had to be some way to take Sam from where he was to where he should be. Sam did not merely run off into the homosexual lifestyle. He felt it was his only alternative. He had misdiagnosed the situation based on the limited information he had at the time. Allow me here to delve into an interesting and important phenomenon that I have discovered with many individuals like Sam.

Definitions

Many who end up "coming out of the closet" feel the need to declare something, but what do they declare if there are only two options? This is where the dilemma gets tricky for people like Sam. He did not originally have a sexual desire toward men, but why does he not desire women? Most of them feel that their diagnosis is an "either/or" proposition. Their options being:

- Gay or straight.
- Homosexual or heterosexual.
- Sex with men or sex with women.

The oversimplified way to describe the biblical alternative is to say "neither." That is not an accurate assessment because it once again puts them into an "outcast" category, and that is something they are not. These are perfectly "normal" people who have been created by God for unique purposes. *It is degrading to categorize them based purely on secular terms.*

For that reason, I see the alternative as not so much an alternative, but a *"definition."* A eunuch is not someone who automatically made a choice between one, two, or even three options. In fact, in most cases, it is not a choice. In others, it was based upon a commitment to Christ. Some, like Sam are *"born that way,"* while others may choose between the following:

- Married or unmarried.
- Sexually pure or sexually abstinent.

Acceptance

A natural eunuch's uniqueness is not a matter of sexual orientation, but a matter of commitment. For Sam, it was not a matter of choices, but one of discovery.

For example, I did not choose to be what I am. I never felt the struggle within me as to my attraction to the opposite sex. I knew early on that I liked girls. My choice was not trying to decide if I liked girls or not. I did. My choice was deciding if I was going to indulge in promiscuity or to stay pure. That is the choice, by the way, all children should be taught that they must one day make. We are *all* to be pure and chaste, no matter whether we desire the opposite sex or not.

I had to decide if I was going to remain chaste until marriage or not. Chastity, however, is not optional for a Christian. We are to keep ourselves sexually pure outside of marriage. For those who choose they are not going to marry, they must decide to remain chaste in an unmarried situation to obey God. The Apostle Paul spoke of this regarding himself, but he also knew that some would not be able to do as he did. His contention was that it was better to marry than to "burn" with desires. Some people have a stronger need for marriage than others. Perhaps I could have stayed unmarried and pure, but I am not certain. For me it was surely better that I marry.

Sam had already stepped over the line of chastity into immorality. Please allow me to clarify this point: I do not believe that Sam was sold to perversion. Some people can become so drawn to the "pleasures of sin," whether it is homosexuality or any other type of sexual addiction and/or practice, that they become addicted. Yes, he had been involved in same-sex behavior, but it was not an overwhelming or uncontrollable desire.

However, like any sin, once we have engaged in it, an appetite begins to develop for that sin. Where there once was no desire, an appetite begins to develop.

There are many people that seem to think there is no coming back from homosexual practices. That is like saying there is no coming back from adultery. There absolutely is forgiveness and a way back from both of these sins. Sam had fallen prey to his fault. What was Sam's fault? It was pride and impatience. It was not homosexuality. If Sam would have waited on the Lord and humbled himself before the Lord, he would not have chosen to do what he knew to be wrong. Sam was not looking to be immoral, but his faults overtook him and led him into an immoral behavior.

So, if many like Sam are not at first sexually attracted to their own sex, why do they fall into homosexuality? I contend that *it is not about attraction, but about acceptance.* Let's use Sam as an example. He would not have found acceptance from Sara had he told her that he was not attracted to her. She would not have understood. He could not explain it to his family or his pastor (although some try) because they would consider him to be strange or perverted. With whom would he find acceptance? He found it with others that were likewise not attracted to women. Unfortunately, in our society, that means those who are involved in the same sex lifestyle. They desire closeness and acceptance, and they find the fulfillment of that desire in the wrong places when they cannot find it among family and friends.

The Deceiver

Sex is perhaps the most powerful drug that Satan uses with young people. When Paul admonished Timothy to flee from youthful lusts, he knew the power of sex in the life of young adults. I am not suggesting that sex cannot be a problem at any age, but Satan wants to steal the chastity of a young person more than anything. He knows that once he can get that hold on us, he can use it against us for the rest of our lives. Satan introduces sex to our kids as young as possible, and he makes it as appealing as possible. He

23

convinces us that we are missing out on something great if we do not indulge ourselves in sex.

Here is the truth: Sex outside of a biblical marriage is a baseless and empty passion. I did not say it was not pleasurable. All sin has pleasure for a season, but sex has a short season. That is why sex creates addiction. We need to repeat the act to satisfy the lust for the pleasure. Within marriage, it is totally satisfying and fulfilling when it is part of a holy relationship. *Marriage is what perfects sex.* Sex does not perfect marriage, but marriage is the outlet for our sexual needs.

Satan wants us to believe that we must have sex, at any cost, in order to be happy. That is such an obvious lie, yet we are often oblivious to Satan's most obvious lies. Many people are miserable in their sexual promiscuity. The nature of promiscuity is something that has no boundaries or limitations. A promiscuous person uses sex outside of its intended purpose for a way to merely fulfill passion or lust. There is no peace or joy in that type of sex. Yet sex permeates all parts of our society as though we cannot be happy without it.

Therefore, as this relates to Sam, we see a young man who has been taught that sex is necessary. He, like all young men, desire closeness with other young guys his age, but he is not attracted to girls. He feels accepted by men who have bought into Satan's lie that sex must be involved. They convince Sam of that same lie, and he is introduced to the intimacy that sex displays. An appetite for this closeness—this intimacy—is created. Once he has partaken, he must have more.

It is not that he began with a sexual desire for men, but that his desire for closeness become fulfilled the wrong way. Some men become involved in same sex activities even after they are older. They might even "prefer" women, but pornography has created a strong desire in them that is not based on attraction, but perversion. These men become attracted to the activity of sexual perversion, even though they are naturally attracted to the opposite sex. The same is true of many women.

Let me take this a step further. Sodom was not merely a city filled with homosexual activity. In fact, there may have been fewer homosexuals than you think. What happened in Sodom and other cultures throughout history was the breakdown of all restraint. Men who were not attracted to men developed appetites for sexual perversions and that led to same sex activities. That is more rampant in America than we know. It might shock you if you knew of the men and women who partake in same sex activities, yet would claim they are attracted to the opposite sex.

Why do I delve into these sexual perversion issues? We must understand that someone like Sam does not start out with a sexual desire for men, but a desire for closeness. Then that desire is expressed and fulfilled in the wrong way, creating an appetite for that fulfillment. I am not saying that the attraction does not eventually come, but it is *not* the same innocent attraction Sam was looking for that night when he went on a date with Sara. He was seeking a pure attraction based on holy desires that would lead to a God-sanctioned and lifelong relationship. This is why so many homosexuals are unable to stay in a relationship for any length of time. Their relationship is based on sexuality rather than on purity.

If someone could have explained to Sam why he felt the way he did after he kissed Sara that night, perhaps everything would have been different. Up until then, Sam's thoughts had been pure. He had not sought to lose that purity, but what he did not realize was that Satan was after him. The way he got to him was through despair and confusion. Sam needed answers, but he did not know where to get them. He was lost and alone. He was not a homosexual, and he was very relieved when he finally realized this fact.

What I showed Sam that night is the basis for the remainder of this book. That night, I presented a scriptural concept to Sam that showed him that he was indeed "born that way," but it was not in the way he feared. He was made by God to be a unique individual with a special calling. That is why it was so important to me that I was prepared to present the truth in a clear and honest manner. The result was amazing and powerful. I saw a young man not only turn away from his sin, but also accept his true purpose. As wonderful as it was to hear him declare his freedom from sin when he said,

"I am not a homosexual," it was thrilling when he realized and confessed his true purpose. Those words still ring in my ears. *"I'm a eunuch."* Sam had found his purpose.

Chapter Four
A NEW JOURNEY

Sam's discovery was two-fold. He first declared what *he was not*, and then declared what *he was*. He had a change of mind and heart. In other words, Sam repented. That was the beginning of the greatest change in Sam's life since the day he was saved. It would be wrong to judge Sam for the sins in which he briefly became involved, because as soon as Sam was presented with the truth, he responded by changing his mind and heart. He then followed through by abandoning the sinful lifestyle and subsequently accepting the life God had planned for him.

Sam's discovery was an amazing moment for me, because it was to be my first real experience teaching someone the truth about eunuchs. For many, the word *eunuch* conjures up strange thoughts and even brings snickers to some. Obviously, the reason for that is the fact that we have accepted the distorted view of eunuchs. I am convinced that Satan (as always) is behind that distortion. How is that roaring lion able to perpetuate homosexuality upon a society? He does it by distorting one truth and then following up that distortion with his own lies.

During the writing of this chapter, the Supreme Court made a monumental decision and overturned the Defense of Marriage Act. How did this nation get to the place where same sex marriage is considered not only a legal right, but in the minds of many, a moral right? It happened because we, who possess the truth, do not know the truth.

To know the truth is to be made free. We cannot help make others free when we are still in the bondage of misinterpretation. The misinterpretation that I refer to here is the truth about what eunuchs are created to be. We have perverted a holy concept, and the results have brought great harm to our nation.

We must come to the knowledge of the truth if we are going to reach this nation with the truth. This truth is not a new truth as much as it is a *lost truth*. It is not a dispensational truth. It is not a truth meant for Christ's time on this earth, but no longer relevant to us today. It still remains true, although not understood and certainly not taught. I did not discover the cure for homosexuality. The only cure for homosexuality is the power of the blood of Christ, like any other sin. I merely found a biblical truth that Satan has craftily hidden from us for centuries.

What Is a Eunuch?

Before we discuss the truth according to the Bible, we need to understand the distortion of this truth. There are three major misinterpretations with how some view biblical eunuchs. I would like to highlight them and expose their flaws.

Eunuchs are not a third gender. Some within Christian circles have tried to re-label eunuchs as a third gender within our society. This is preposterous. Every human-being fits within God's original creation story. In the beginning, Genesis chapter 1, we read, *"In the image of God created He him; male and female created He them."* Throughout Scripture, we find no alternative to God's original creation. Quite the opposite, we find gender roles that fit perfectly with God's created binary system. They are clearly seen:

- Male and Female
- Man and Woman
- Husband and Wife
- Father and Mother
- Son and Daughter
- Boy and Girl
- Uncle and Aunt
- Bridegroom and Bride
- King and Queen
- Him and Her
- He and She

28

Eunuchs are not same-sex lovers. Though, as we have seen already, some eunuchs may end up sexually confused in this area. The fact remains that they are not "homosexual." In fact, the word *eunuch* dispels sexual activity.

Eunuchs cannot be confined to mean only those who have been castrated. What do you think of when you hear the word eunuch? Do you instantly think "guardian," "nurturer," or "officer"? I am certain that none of those words come to mind. In fact, if you are like the majority of people when you hear the word eunuch, you immediately assume it's defining a man who has been castrated or emasculated. This definition, however, is *only secondary* to the primary meaning for the word eunuch.

The scriptural description and display of eunuchs is quite interesting. In the Old Testament, the Hebrew word from which eunuch is translated is the word *saris*, pronounced saw-reese. The first mention of this word, ironically, is found in Genesis chapter 39. In verse 1 of Genesis 39, we are introduced to a man by the name of Potiphar, "an officer of Pharaoh."

The word "officer" here is simply another English translation for the Hebrew word *saris*, or eunuch. It's worthy to note that the first mention of a eunuch in the Bible is a man who certainly does not fit the modern day stereotype that is often connected to the word eunuch. I say this for two reasons: Potiphar *had a wife,* and he was a *high level servant in the kingdom.* From this, we can certainly see that, according to Scripture, a eunuch was not necessarily one who had been castrated.

Take a look at some of the words God associates with eunuchs:

- *Officer in the kingdom* and *captain of the guard* ~ Genesis.39:1
- *Guardian of the women* and *very kind* ~ Esther 2:1-10
- *Nurturers, tender, loving, brave* and *friendly* ~ Daniel 1:1-11
- *Caretakers for soldiers, bodyguards for king* ~ Jeremiah 52:1-27

Apparently, God's Word pays high regard to those men who bore the title of eunuch. The only exception was for those who had actually been physically castrated. According to Jewish custom, it was unlawful for a man to enter the temple if he was a eunuch due to self-mutilation, war, or injury. It displeased God to see His people imitate the heathen nations and their practices. One of the greatest and most heinous acts of the heathen was self-mutilation. This act, taken upon children, made God angry. He forbade His people from adopting these practices and made the penalty steep.

Some modern commentaries claim the natural eunuch is a person born with a birth-defect. This birth-defect theory is unfortunate and incorrect. For the most part, this theory derives from a contemporary explanation that ignores historical commentary, grammatical hermeneutics, and the simplicity of Scripture. As a result, the truth has been distorted and hidden from recent generations. More details and commentary are provided later as we consider the honorable heritage of eunuchism, but here are some historical comments related to the natural eunuch.

Historical Commentary

Disclaimer: The quotes from the men below are not a declaration of our personal agreement with their doctrinal positions, but rather as proof that the subject of eunuchism is not a new idea or teaching.

Basilides, disciple of Saint Matthew and Christian Teacher, 117-138 AD, *The Library of Christian Classics*, Basilides-Matt.19:12

"Some men from the womb have a *nature* to turn away from women, and those who are subject to this natural constitution do well not to marry. These are the eunuchs who are not unable, but unwilling, they are thus gifted."

Philo Judaeus, Jewish Historian, 25 BC-50 AD, *The Works of Philo*: page 436: X11

"A natural eunuch: a man skillful in affairs of state is truly a eunuch, *having in appearance, indeed, the organs of generation, but being deprived of all the motivation requisite for generating*" That is certainly plain and straightforward enough, but that isn't all, Philo then compares the condition of the natural eunuch to a man who has two eyes, yet, sees differently than everyone else. Furthermore, during Philo's lifetime a natural eunuch was permitted under the law to marry a woman for public stature and/or political reasons, whereas a castrated eunuch was not."

John Calvin, 16th century religious leader, *Calvin Commentary*, Mat. 19:11-12

"The gift of born celibacy is a special gift; for when (Christ) says that all are not capable of receiving it, but those to whom it is given, he plainly shows that it was not given to all." Calvin further states: "while some men are by nature fit to marry, though they abstain, they do not tempt God, because God grants them exemption."

C.H. Spurgeon, 19th century pastor, *Exposition to the Gospel of Matthew*—Chapter 19

"Some have but *feeble desires* concerning marriage (relations) and they were so born. They will find it good to remain as they are."

John Wesley, 18th century Methodist leader, Wesley's Explanatory Notes—Matthew 19:11-12

"To whom is given this excellent gift of God (?) Now this is given to three sorts of persons to some by *natural constitution*, without their choice: to others by violence, against their choice; and to others by grace with their choice: who steadily withstand their natural inclinations that they may wait upon God without distraction."

Grammatical Hermeneutics

Study the language of Matthew 19, Jesus is speaking from the standpoint of design and purpose; "from the beginning" and "from the womb." It is also interesting that the Greek word translated "womb" in Matthew 19:12 is the same word in John 7:38 used to describe the inner man or soul of a person. Culturally, Jews of that day considered marriage and the bearing of children to be a duty. Even then it appears they ignored the unmarried status of many heroes of the faith such as Jeremiah, Daniel, and Elijah, to name a few. The unmarried Jesus would have also been a rare exception

31

in that day and culture. For sure, marriage is certainly the norm, but as Paul explains in 1 Corinthians 7, both the married life and the unmarried life are gifts from God.

Simplicity of Scripture

As you can see, many problems exist for those who insist on the "birth-defect" interpretation, but one glaring example is the case of the third eunuch. If one insists that the term "eunuch" can only be defined in terms of castration, then one must concede that the third eunuch who chose the life of a eunuch must have also practiced self-mutilation. Of course, such self-mutilation is strictly against the precepts of God's Word.

The term eunuch is quite simply defined by Christ to encompass three distinct persons. The difference between the first eunuch mentioned by Christ and the second eunuch is indeed the process of *becoming*. There is a difference between he who *is* a eunuch and he who *becomes* a eunuch. Furthermore, if the "born" eunuch and the "made" eunuch were both impotent, then logically we would only have two kind of eunuchs—those capable and those incapable of a physical relationship. Yet, Christ makes a clear distinction between *three* types of eunuchs.

What Jesus Taught

According to *Matthew 19:10-12*, there were *three types of eunuchs.* Below, you will find each type listed alongside their original biblical definition in accordance with the language Jesus spoke.

God-Made Eunuchs: Those who are born that way "from their mother's womb" (created by God with no sexual desire toward the opposite sex).

The word Jesus used in His language to denote this type of eunuch is *eunouchos*. *Eunouchos* – literally, "alone in bed."

Man-Made Eunuchs: Those who are made eunuchs of men. (*Male organs literally cut away as a child. I also believe that if an unnatural relationship or any form of sexual abuse has taken place with a child, it could produce this type of eunuch.*) This type of eunuch is a sad case. These dear eunuchs are made eunuchs due to war, molestation, castration, or in some instances, medical malpractice.

The word Jesus used in His language to denote this type of eunuch is *eunouxízō*. *Eunouxízō* – literally, make someone a eunuch; to emasculate (castrate). Transliteration: eunouchizó. Phonetic spelling: yoo-noo-khid'-zo.

Self-Made Eunuchs: Those who make themselves eunuchs for the kingdom of heaven's sake (consumed with the Kingdom of God). These blessed few are those Christians who desire to work for God without dealing with the distractions associated with marriage—a spiritual castration not a physical one.

The word Jesus used in His language to denote this type of eunuch is *eunoúxos*. *Eunoúxos* – literally, a *castrated* (emasculated) man; a *eunuch*; 'a chamberlain, keeper of the bed-chamber' of an Eastern potentate, a eunuch; (figuratively) someone who *abstains from marriage* (sexual relations) to be *solely devoted to God* (*eunoúxos*) (souter); refers to someone who has chosen to live in *sexual abstinence.*

Jesus spoke with such clarity about this matter, yet it has been clouded among many Christians for centuries. Perhaps, it is because we are not as curious as the disciples were to know the Lord's wishes and teaching. Let me tell the story from this passage so we can understand the context.

Right after Jesus had been transfigured, He began to teach His disciples on a number of topics as you will see in Matthew 17 and 18. Afterward, Jesus went back to the coasts of Judea. As usual, a great multitude of people followed Him and He healed many of them. As usual, the Pharisees were close at hand, watching Him and listening to His teachings, hoping to find something...anything to use against Him.

At the beginning of chapter 19, we hear them speak up on divorce, which was a subject that they thought might do the trick. Divorce seems to be a subject that people like to bring up as a way to trip up our faith. Notice what the Scriptures have to say: *"The Pharisees also came unto him, tempting him, and saying unto him, Is it lawful for a man to put away his wife for every cause?"*

Jesus explained to them the truth about divorce. In so doing, it caused the disciples some serious concern. In a manner of speaking, they wondered if it was even "worth the trouble" to get married. Notice what they asked Him, *"His disciples say unto him, If the case of the man be so with his wife, it is not good to marry."*

Jesus then began to share with them the truths that would lead to His discussion of eunuchs. Jesus was always practical. He never sidestepped a subject, nor did He sugarcoat it. He knew that some could stay pure outside of marriage and He also knew that it would be better for them if they did remain unmarried. Jesus said, *"But he said unto them, All men cannot receive this saying, save they to whom it is given."*

Now, look at His words carefully. He was not referring to what He had said before, but to what He was *about* to say. It was then He spoke clearly about the matter of eunuchs: *"For there are some eunuchs, which were so born from their mother's womb: and there are some eunuchs, which were made eunuchs of men: and there be eunuchs, which have made themselves eunuchs for the kingdom of heaven's sake."*

Jesus was never careless in His words or in the order of His words. He did not begin with the definition we know today of eunuchs. He began by acknowledging those who were born that way. He then spoke of those who were eunuchs in the flesh. He concluded by speaking of those who, like many, chose not to marry for the sake of the faith.

Notice how He concluded this conversation: *"He that is able to receive it, let him receive it."* He encouraged them to accept this as a way of life, if they felt they could. It was not a command, but rather an alternative, if they felt it was something they could accomplish. More important to Him, than choosing to be eunuchs, was that he wanted them to be sexually pure, and if that meant getting married, then so be it. At that point, the conversation was over.

It would be easy, yet foolish, to see this brief dialogue as merely a snippet that had little significance. This was a big deal to these men. Jesus used great care to instruct them well. In the midst of these words, we are faced with the reality that some people are born eunuchs: *"so born from their mother's womb."*

So, for the purpose of our study here, a natural eunuch is born physiologically capable of performing sexual acts, but without natural or unnatural sexual desires. That is not to say that unnatural desires cannot be developed. They absolutely can. For example, we were not born with a desire to drink fermented drinks or to inhale tobacco, but there are many who have developed unnatural desires for these things, and the result is detrimental.

Addictions are usually the perversion of appetite or the development of an unnatural appetite. Many in the "gay" lifestyle are addicted to that which is not natural, and I believe that many of them have this addiction because they were deceived by Satan as to how they were created by God.

A Better Name

Isaiah 56:3-5 – *Neither let the son of the stranger, that hath joined himself to the LORD, speak, saying, The LORD hath utterly separated me from his people: neither let the eunuch say, Behold, I am a dry tree. 4 For thus saith the LORD unto the eunuchs that keep my sabbaths, and choose the things that please me, and take hold of my covenant; 5 Even unto them will I give in mine house and within my walls a place and a name better than of sons and of daughters: I will give them an everlasting name, that shall not be cut off.*

The promises in this passage are most startling. God will give eunuchs who choose the things that please Him a place and a name that is <u>better</u> than those of sons and daughters!

Apparently, in God's eyes, there is much more to a eunuch than just someone who does not perform sexually or someone who doesn't get married. God treats the concept of the eunuch like He would a calling from Him—like a call into the ministry. Let's be honest; if you substitute the word "eunuch" in those verses for the word "pastor," how many sermons would we hear on them? Quite a few, no doubt, but because it uses the word "eunuch," we never hear sermons preached from this passage.

If God calls people to be eunuchs, then the greatest mistake we make as fellow Christians is not to recognize this fact. We believe God calls people to pastor, to serve, to go specific places, and even to get married. Why wouldn't God call people—from the womb—to be eunuchs?

Eunuchs are men and women called to be married to Christ. They aren't meant to get married to someone of the opposite gender. They are meant to serve God in a specific and special way. They do not have the "normal" sexual urges for the opposite gender—and if the truth be told, they (in the beginning) don't have the sexual urges for the same gender either.

A eunuch, therefore, is a calling (and for some a choice) to serve God and God alone—someone dedicated to service.

As mentioned already, the term "eunuch" in the Old Testament comes from the Hebrew word "saris," pronounced "saw-reese." Let's take a look at the word in greater detail. This word is translated a variety of ways in the Old Testament such as "officer" (1 Samuel 8:15) and "chamberlain" (Esther 1:10). It is also left un-translated once with an additional word as "rab saris," which means "chief eunuch."

The following is a list of Biblical references where you can find the Hebrew word "saris":

- Genesis 37:36; 39:1; 40:2; 40:7
- 1 Samuel 8:15
- 1 Kings 22:9
- 2 Kings 8:6; 9:32; 18:17; 20:18; 23:11; 24:12; 24:15; 25:19
- 1 Chronicles 28:1
- 2 Chronicles 18:8
- Esther 1:10; 1:12; 1:15; 2:3; 2:14; 2:15; 2:21; 4:4; 4:5; 6:2; 6:14; 7:9
- Isaiah 39:7; 56:3; 56:4

36

- Jeremiah 29:2; 34:19; 38:7; 39:3; 39:13; 41:16; 52:25
- Daniel 1:3; 1:7; 1:8; 1:9; 1:10; 1:11; 1:18

The primary meaning for a eunuch is not a castrated male, but more often a dedicated keeper or guardian. The biblical context will tell us if the eunuch is a commander, doorkeeper, or some other occupation.

For example, in Genesis 39:1, it tells us that Potiphar was an "officer" of Pharaoh. Specifically, he was a commander in Pharaoh's guard who had a variety of duties, including that of oversight of political prisoners and Pharaoh's personal prison. It literally tells us that he was a eunuch, dedicated to the service of Pharaoh. However, there is no evidence he was castrated—he even had a wife.

Some Old Testament eunuchs were never castrated and were called such only because they were reserved to be dedicated servants to a particular cause or person. Daniel is an example of this. He and many other young, unmarried men were turned over to the chief of eunuchs (Daniel 1:3-4). Of this group, the king wanted the best of the best to be prepared for dedicated service to the throne—those who were unblemished. *Castration would have negated this qualification. They were unblemished—not castrated.*

The only sure way for a reader to know whether a certain biblical eunuch is castrated would be if some other words are used to convey such.

In short, a good way to understand the word "eunuch" would be thus: An individual who is *chosen for* or *chosen to be a dedicated servant to a cause or a person.*

Why Would God Create or Call Eunuchs?

Undoubtedly, the first question many Christians who come to understand this is: "Why would God create or call eunuchs at all? What's the point?" It's a fair question.

To begin with, there are clearly times and circumstances where the calling of a eunuch has vast advantages over married individuals. 1 Corinthians, chapter 7 gives us direction in this regard. The chapter begins with a discussion on marriage, but right in the middle of it, Paul makes a remarkable statement:

1 Corinthians 7:7-9 – *For I would that all men were even as I myself. But every man hath his proper gift of God, one after this manner, and another after that. 8 I say therefore to the unmarried and widows, It is good for them if they abide even as I. 9 But if they cannot contain, let them marry: for it is better to marry than to burn.*

Paul was unmarried—he was single. He makes the intriguing statement that he wished that all men would remain single—not get married at all! He qualifies it by saying that not everyone would be able to do so, and if someone did choose to get married, they would not be sinning. But Paul felt it better that Christians of his day did not get married.

Paul gives two reasons why he recommends Christians to remain unmarried.

Reason One

The first reason has to do with the circumstances that Christianity labored under. It was a distressful time…a time of persecution, of bloodshed, of torture, and of execution. He says:

1 Corinthians 7:25-27 – *Now concerning virgins I have no commandment of the Lord: yet I give my judgment, as one that hath obtained mercy of the Lord to be faithful. 26 I suppose therefore that <u>this is good for the present distress</u>, I say, that it is good for a man so to be. 27 Art thou bound unto a wife? seek not to be loosed. Art thou loosed from a wife? seek not a wife.*

Because of the difficulties of being a Christian in that era, Paul felt that Christians would be more faithful to God if they did not have the burden of a marriage. If someone held a gun to your head and said:

"Renounce Christ or I'll blow your brains out," you might have enough faith and trust in God to reply, "Pull the trigger." But what if someone held the same gun to your spouse's head or your child's and said, "Renounce

Christ or I'll blow their brains out"? Ah! Now the decision is significantly more difficult.

It may very well be that during times of heavy persecution, God calls more eunuchs to His cause. A eunuch, without the burden, cares, and problems of a marriage, can focus all of his attention on serving Christ.

In this context, no wonder God would lavish a better name on these individuals! They are called to a special service—maybe during times of great distress.

Reason Two

1 Corinthians 7:28 – *But and if thou marry, thou hast not sinned; and if a virgin marry, she hath not sinned. Nevertheless <u>such shall have trouble in the flesh</u>: but I spare you.*

1 Corinthians 7:32-35 – *But I would have you without carefulness. He that is unmarried careth for the things that belong to the Lord, how he may please the Lord: 33 But <u>he that is married careth for the things that are of the world</u>, how he may please his wife. 34 There is difference also between a wife and a virgin. The unmarried woman careth for the things of the Lord, that she may be holy both in body and in spirit: but she that is married careth for the things of the world, how she may please her husband. 35 And this I speak for your own profit; not that I may cast a snare upon you, but for that which is comely, and that ye may attend upon the Lord without distraction.*

Eunuchs have the unique distinction and position to focus all their energy on the Lord. And from our experiences working with eunuchs, they tend to be more sold-out for the cause of Christ than many other Christians. They simply don't have the distractions that a married man or woman has. They can throw all their energy and care before the Lord without the cares that a married man or woman may deal with every day.

There is absolutely nothing wrong with marriage. Paul makes that abundantly clear. But, too, there is nothing wrong with being called a eunuch for Christ—to give one's self wholly over to the work of the Lord.

What church would not love to have a large group of these individuals serving with and among them? This was exactly what the early church fathers and great men of God throughout history have taught and preached. Find these people that God has chosen as eunuchs and let them be used in ministry for His service and for His glory.

Some practice celibacy because they were created for it, and others practice it of their own free will. But regardless, eunuchs have a special place in God's order.

Some Familiar Eunuchs in Scripture

Male eunuchs were trusted around married women. They were never a threat to holy matrimony. They were loyal, royal guardians and household nurturers. They were dedicated servants—often lifelong servants—to a cause or to a person. They were called eunuchs.

The following is a list of men and women who would be considered biblical eunuchs. In the vast majority of cases, they were all faithfully unmarried individuals dedicated to a cause, person, or purpose. Potiphar is the most notable exception to this, but we do not know the circumstances behind his marriage. We do know that he was a dedicated servant to Pharaoh and, as such, fits every other qualification of being a eunuch. Here is the list:

Miriam, the sister of Moses, helped organize Israelite women into the first choir recorded in the Bible.

Elijah, the most influential prophet of Israel, spent most of his life seeing to the needs of the northern Kingdom of Israel.

Elisha was mentored by Elijah, and he succeeded Elijah as prophet to the Kingdom of Israel. He was probably the most Christ-like prophet of the Old Testament. He practiced New Testament virtues, like giving his enemy food and water.

Jeremiah was specifically ordered by God not to marry (Jeremiah 16:1-2). He preached for about 50 years, leading up to the destruction of Jerusalem by the Babylonian army.

Daniel was one of a handful of people in Scripture of whom nothing negative is written. Like Joseph before him, Daniel became a master of dreams with prophetic overtones. The book named after him has become indispensable to students and scholars of Bible prophecy. The story of Daniel in the Lion's Den is perhaps one of the most famous stories told to children. Daniel served at least three separate kings during his lifetime— not to mention staying true to God throughout all of it.

Shadrach, Meshach, and Abednego, commonly known as "The Three Hebrew Children," displayed bravery and courageous devotion to the Lord in the face of being burned to death. These three young men were miraculously delivered by God from King Nebuchadnezzar's fiery furnace. They served as officers and princes in Babylon.

John the Baptist was cousin to Jesus and six months older than Jesus. John was much like Elijah—removed from people, very pointed and confrontational in his preaching. His purpose in life was to prepare the nation of Israel for the arrival of the Messiah and to introduce the Savior to the world. His greatest honor was to baptize Jesus Christ in the Jordan River. He served God faithfully until his death.

The Apostle John authored five books and letters of the New Testament, including the Gospel of John and the prophetic book of Revelation, the last book of the Bible. His main themes were truth, light, and love. He became known as the Apostle of Love. It was he who leaned against Jesus' breast. And of all the disciples, only he was to be found near the Cross. Jesus tasked him with the service of caring for His mother. History tells us that only John remained unmarried throughout his life and that he was the last of the New Testament apostles to die.

The Apostle Paul was by far the most accomplished Christian of the New Testament, surpassing even the first apostles who physically walked with Jesus Christ. He wrote half of the New Testament twenty seven books and letters, and he became the most successful missionary and church planter in history.

Barnabas was the man credited with being the first to accept and trust Paul while the church was still skeptical of the man who at one time harassed and killed Christians before he was converted. Barnabas mentored Paul, gave him credibility, and went with Paul on the first missionary journey, planting several churches among the Gentiles.

Timothy became Paul's most trusted spiritual son. He was the biracial son of a Greek father and a Jewish mother. As a youth, Timothy became an able Christian leader, who pastored the famous Church of Ephesus—the same church pastored by John the Beloved and the same church where Mary the mother of Jesus was a member.

Lydia was a wealthy business woman who accommodated Paul and his missionary team in the city of Philippi. Lydia became a charter member of the Philippian Church, and she was probably a leader there.

Jesus Christ, The most famous faithfully unmarried person ever. He should be the number one role model of what it means to live the unmarried life. As we follow Christ, let's remember that our Lord was *physically* unmarried. This historical fact should motivate every church to find ways to make "singles"—*honorable, wholly dedicated, life-long unmarried individuals*—an important part of their ministry, rather than unintentionally sidelining them in good efforts to promote marriage.

All of us, eventually, will in a way become eunuchs when we get to heaven. No one will be physically married, and everyone will be wholly dedicated to God for eternity:

Luke 20:34-35 – *And Jesus answering said unto them, The children of this world marry, and are given in marriage: But they which shall be accounted worthy to obtain that world, and the resurrection from the dead, neither marry, nor are given in marriage.*

Wrong Perspectives

Unfortunately, Christians have allowed Satan to steal a concept that Jesus taught clearly to His disciples. The indoctrination begins from the time a child is small. We teach little boys that *their purpose* in life is to marry, and we teach our little girls that *their purpose* in life is to be a wife and mother. We make marriage a badge of honor rather than a choice of honoring God. When is the last time you heard a sermon on why it is better to remain unmarried?

Individuals like Sam sit in our churches feeling that the only way they can be complete is by being married, but that is not what Jesus taught. The reason we have few eunuchs in the faith is because we have made *remaining unmarried* a stigma in our churches. An unmarried person often feels like a second class citizen and a dysfunctional person. That leads to two problems. It causes people to marry someone out of desperation when they have no real reason to marry. It also leads some who have no sexual desire to turn to a lifestyle they otherwise would never have chosen or even considered.

Being unmarried does not make an individual a second class Christian. Imagine if Sam had heard this taught in Sunday school and church when he was growing up. Imagine if Sam had seen men and women who had chosen to remain unmarried, eunuchs, who were honored for their commitment to Christ. Perhaps he could have avoided unnecessary heartbreak. Knowing the circumstances, it helps me to understand why Sam chose the path he followed. I find it impossible to imagine that he has forfeited his usefulness for God as a result of his foray into a life for which he saw no other alternative.

Jesus never went around asking, "Do you have a boyfriend?" Nor did He make quips or suggestions that everyone should be looking for a wife. Finding a spouse was not a main topic for Him, so why is it for us? We have created a society that feels incomplete without a spouse. Thus we have husbands emotionally draining wives and wives emotionally draining husbands, all in an attempt to find the security they should already have in their walk with the Lord. The emphasis on marriage within the Christian community is somewhat to blame for the issue of same sex marriage. We have made people who remain unmarried and chaste to be abnormal.

Right Perspectives

Everyone should be taught the principles regarding eunuchs. Our young people should be given the liberty to remain unmarried, if they choose. The issue of homosexuality is not the most difficult issue confronting our churches today, not by a long shot. However, it is a byproduct of the issue that *is* our most difficult issue. Divorce is one of the biggest problems we face today. We treat those who have experienced divorce in much the same way we treat those who have gone off into the gay lifestyle. Both are influenced by the lack of teaching that we have done on this subject.

Why could there not be ministries where unmarried individuals rejoice over their position and are encouraged for choosing to remain unmarried? Instead, the ministries that do exist are perceived as a place for "losers" to grieve over the fact that they could not find a spouse. Other ministries are advertised as the place to find a spouse, a meat market so to speak. Perhaps those who feel no attraction whatsoever, those who have not "settled" for the next person to come along, or those who were *born that way,* should be given far greater honor and attention than we have given them.

We are quick to teach what God said to Adam in the Garden, but totally negligent to teach what Jesus taught in Matthew 19. Is marriage then an unnecessary thing? Absolutely not... it can be necessary, if someone feels they cannot serve the Lord unmarried. Many women are born with a natural inclination to be a wife and mother, and that is obviously the purpose for which they were created, but not all. I have found that some lesbians are women who did not have those desires. They did not find the thought of being married a thing they desired. But our culture has made them to feel they are missing out on something. As a result, they have turned to the gay lifestyle to fulfill what Satan has convinced them they are missing.

Some men are born with a strong need to have a wife. Many men are naturally more sexually needy than women, thus they need to get married in order to satisfy those needs. When that kind of man marries a wife, the Bible says he has found a good thing. In that situation, they understand their needs and purpose, and the chances are greater that they will remain married. However, now they have entered into a contract that is binding in the sight of God. Why do we rush our young people to enter into such a binding agreement so carelessly without ever giving them the right to remain *faithfully unmarried?*

Some parents may be as unhappy about their child being unmarried as they would if they became gay. They fear for them to be alone or not to have children. Or perhaps they are afraid of not having grandchildren to brag about and enjoy. We have created a societal pressure that promotes marriage over remaining unmarried. Although the Bible says that marriage is honorable, that does not mean that being unmarried is not equally honorable, if that is what God wants for a person.

Sam was part of a Christian world that behaved as though marriage was the only acceptable choice, so he was forced to try to be something he was not. In most churches, people like Sam feel pressured to date and find a wife. What if there were classes for those who are honorably unmarried? Perhaps these people could find a group where they could feel accepted. How about a class that deals with the issues of being unmarried with the right perspectives that provides a choice and teaches that being unmarried is possibly the will of God for a person's life?

Cause and Cure

Why is "homosexuality" running rampant in this day? Perhaps the cause is also the cure. In the past, before it was "acceptable" to be "gay," we had men and women that were born to be eunuchs. These men and women felt pressure to be married, so they succumbed to an unhappy scriptural marriage with someone they did not desire. They continued in their marriage because it was unacceptable to be divorced, but when divorce became less of a stigma, many of them ultimately chose divorce. They determined that the marriage had failed because they had chosen the *wrong person.* They did not realize it was because they were born to be unmarried. They were trying to create desires that did not exist. They were trying to accomplish what society imposed on them. So, they remarried, leading many to another bad marriage. Still unable to find fulfillment in a scriptural marriage, many chose same sex relationships. Satan convinced them that the problem was that they were attracted to their own sex. When in reality they were not attracted to either sex. They were eunuchs. *God is not interested in rescuing anyone from their true sexual identity. On the contrary, God desires to rescue people from rooting their true identity in sexuality.*

Unfortunately, the same problems that led to many bad marriages in the past also influenced the creation of the openly gay lifestyle we see today. Since we have promoted marriage as "the thing to do," many of them decided they must have the right to marry within the gay lifestyle. Please get this: *marriage does not legitimize their sexuality, it legitimizes them personally.* That is what we taught them. Today, they do not feel like a functional, adequate, normal adult, without being married. *It is becoming more unnatural to be unmarried, than it is to be married to the wrong sex.*

The solution for many of our problems is found in Matthew 19, yet we have ignored it far too long. We must face the fact that there are untold numbers of people who are eunuchs by choice, but have never been defined as such. We must also conclude that those chosen by God to be eunuchs is far higher than we may have thought. Many have married out of social pressure. Some have remained unmarried and chaste. Others live in fornication, seeking fulfillment outside of a committed relationship for which they have no desire. Finally, there are others who are drawn into the "gay" lifestyle where they assume they "fit in."

My eunuch friend, let me assure you that you are not alone. Perhaps you have made mistakes out of ignorance, but you must decide now what you are going to do with the truth you have been given. You can do as Sam did and repent. That does not mean you must put on sackcloth and ashes and grovel at the altar in some church to atone for your sin. It requires two steps, and they are the steps Sam took that night when he was first given the light of the truth.

Declare the truth that you are not a homosexual.

Declare the truth that you are a eunuch.

From here – a new journey for Christ begins. See it for the wonderful life it was meant to be, because after all, *you were chosen by God to be "born that way."*

Chapter Five
TRUTH AND LIES: SAME SEX ATTRACTIONS

The question Sam dealt with as a teenager was not an attraction to the same sex, but why he was not attracted to the opposite sex. He had not even seriously considered the idea that he may have a same sex attraction until confronted with that possibility in college. In fact, many homosexuals actually affirm to have had *no sexual desire* before they gravitated toward an *unnatural sexual desire.*

Why then, do some claim to have had *same sex attractions* for as long as they can remember? Why do some people claim to have been born as a homosexual? In light of Matthew 19:12, the answer is not as overwhelming as you might think. Several things make up the premise for this explanation.

God's Word identifies some as having been born with no sexual desire toward the opposite sex.

Individuals *born that way* generally can be described as caring, nurturing, affectionate, and friendly.

Societal and church-related peer pressure often stigmatize the born eunuch, thus causing negative decisions to be made, which can include *getting married* to appease others or to *"fix the problem."* For others, they make pendulum decisions and *declare themselves "gay,"* while a few more, in utter depression, escape through suicide.

Why Am I Attracted to the Same Sex?

This is the question I am asked by many eunuchs. While they recognize the truth of what the Bible says and have acknowledged their own standing as a eunuch, they are often still confused as to why God would allow them to be attracted to the same sex. During the course of identifying biblical-eunuchs, on occasion, we hear a testimony that goes something like this: *"From the beginning I was always different. I never got along well with guys my age and felt more comfortable around girls. I think my first crush was on a boy. My first sexual longings were directed not at girls, but at boys. I was never attracted to girls."*

It is not my desire or intention to argue with another person's feelings. I have not been in their position, so I cannot know what feelings they experience. However, if we look at this closer and objectively, perhaps we can have a better understanding. Here are three types of same sex attraction that we need to consider:

1. Inherent same sex attraction. A sexual "attraction" is simply a hunger. It could be a natural or unnatural emotional appetite. Everyone has emotional and spiritual hunger.

Proverbs 13:25 – *The righteous eateth to the satisfying of his soul: but the belly of the wicked shall want.*

This hunger could be good or bad. For example, we are all created with a natural hunger to ingest food—this is good. Food strengthens us and keeps us healthy. We are not created with a hunger to ingest cocaine—it is unnatural. Any unnatural hunger is the result of a deranged appetite. How did Jacob steal Esau's birthright? In Genesis chapter 25, we find that Esau lost his birthright because Jacob took advantage of his hunger. The craziest part is that Esau was given soup, and he didn't even really like soup. The Bible is clear to mention that he was a meat eater. Jacob "stole" Esau's birthright with food that Esau didn't even care for—talk about adding insult to injury. Satan too will do his best to manipulate your appetite when he sees you are hungry. A person hungry for love and acceptance will more than likely be tempted with sex. Satan desperately wants a person to trade

50

their purity for pleasure. The hunger for love isn't a bad thing as long as we fill the hunger the right way. Imitation love will always end badly. Once a person acquires a taste for a negative or unnatural appetite, hunger pangs will exist, begging you to satisfy the pain or lust. No one has hunger pangs for the unnatural until they experience a taste of the unnatural.

Same sex attraction is not exclusive. We all possess it. It is inherent in every young boy to feel an attraction for closeness to other boys as well as to grown men. It is inherent in every young girl to be attracted to other young girls, as well as older women. That has nothing to do with sex. It is a part of making us who we are eventually going to become. Every little boy is attracted to male leadership and mentorship. Every little girl is likewise attracted to adult women who become teachers, leaders and role models.

We can all remember the special bond we felt with adults of the same sex, and while we are also attracted to the opposite sex, it was a different type of attraction. I have a special place in my heart for the men with whom I built strong relationships with as a boy. Many of them became role models or mentors.

As a young boy, I also wanted to be close to other boys, which was in no way a strange attraction. It is perfectly normal for children to be attracted to their own sex and have a desire to be close to them. It is not sexual in a child, because physiologically and hormonally they are too young. It is normal for children to have a longing for same sex closeness. We are created by Almighty God with a desire for close, personal friendships with the same sex. There is nothing wrong, unnatural, or perverted with that type of desire. Every person coming of age experiences this desire for same sex closeness.

The question is whether or not it is the same attraction for eunuchs as it is for others. I have concluded that it is not. Often, those who were born as eunuchs have more difficulty relating to (and with) those of the same sex who are not also eunuchs. This leads me to conclude that we should have biblical eunuchs of both sexes in our churches that interact with the kids. These individuals should be selected and screened with the exact same scrutiny we would any other worker, no more and no less. If a young man sees an adult man who is unmarried, he has someone with whom he can relate, and the same is true with young ladies.

A eunuch male may feel uncomfortable with a man who is married or extremely "macho," because he feels that he cannot relate to him. He may avoid that man and become reclusive. The opportunity for young ladies to find an unmarried lady role model appears to be greater than for boys to find an unmarried man to be their role model. In many walks of life, including church ministries, we have fewer unmarried men than women. That can leave a huge void for some young men in the church.

Born eunuchs also tend to be less comfortable with their same sex peers who are more masculine boys or more feminine girls. These young people often become loners as the years of puberty begin. If we can educate and change the way society looks at these young people in the future, perhaps they will no longer feel excluded and alone.

Dating pressures can prove to be difficult for them. As Satan encourages earlier and earlier sexual awareness in kids, these born eunuchs become isolated much more quickly. When I was a young man, we were all friends far into the teenage years. In spite of the fact that I liked girls, there was not as much pressure placed upon us in the early years to date. Certainly there were those who started dating early, but most of us remained friends.

2. Sexual same sex attraction. Sexual attraction comes from sexual awareness, which often comes from sexual pressure. Young people will often do things they otherwise would not do just to be accepted. When I was a kid, I tried my first cigarette, and I hated it. In fact, adults that began smoking at a young age will usually state that they did not like it at first, but did it to be accepted. The "taste" or attraction to smoking was developed over time. The initial attraction was not smoking, but pleasing their friends.

Today, young people are influenced at a young age to "try" sex. They are then forced to deal with the question of attraction. If a young man is not attracted to girls, then he must be "gay," or if a girl is not attracted to boys,

52

she must be a "lesbian." The peer pressure for sex leads to peer pressure to declare their sexuality. Some (especially girls) who feel the need to leave the "door open" declare themselves as "bi-sexual." It is not about attraction, it is about pressure. There are several important facts regarding this subject of sexual same sex attraction.

Same sex attraction and sexual attraction are two completely different things. This is important. Many young adults are convinced by others that they must be gay because they had same sex desires (for closeness) when they were young. What these "victims" do not understand is that we all had those desires. Just because they had a desire for same sex closeness when they were in first grade does not mean they are gay. All first grade boys have those attractions. Boys have best friends who are boys and girls have best friends who are girls, and those friendships have nothing to do with sexuality.

Sexual longings are not necessarily a sign of attraction, as much as they are of hormones. Sometimes, the hormones of a young person begin to rage early and they begin to long for sex. They should put so much energy into their studies and youthful activities to sufficiently dissipate those longings. Unfortunately, they are often encouraged to consider their sexuality at a young age and they determine they are sexually attracted to the same sex. That is not a subject young people should be forced to deal with at such an early age.

Idleness and exposure are two ways Satan works these hormones into his favor. He exposes young people to sexuality early, and then, in idleness, they begin to think of sex. Because many homes are not vibrant places of family activities, these young people spend endless hours alone in their rooms looking at and thinking about things that corrupt their minds.

Young people can often and easily confuse the desire for "*intimacy*" with a desire for "*sexuality.*" This is a time when a young person is breaking away from their parents and seeking intimacy with another.

"If... THEN" is a terrible way to decide that we are sexually attracted to the same sex. If I am *not* attracted to the *opposite sex... THEN* I am gay...

53

Sexual development comes at different times for everyone. Some young men have been so involved in sports or other activities that their real attraction for girls does not come until they enter college or even later.

Curiosity is not the same as attraction. Let us remember the smoking analogy. Many young people smoke because it looks cool. They are curious, so they try it. If they smoke long enough, a *taste* for it is *acquired*, and eventually an *addiction*. Some young men and women try same sex experiments because they are curious. If they engage in this behavior long enough, they too will eventually develop a taste for unnatural sex and eventually an addiction to it. Undisciplined curiosity breeds confusion. Confusion breeds chaos, and the devil loves chaos.

Attraction is not orientation. Orientation is the way we are made. Men were never oriented for men and women were never oriented for women. Attraction is sensual and sensual is not definitive.

Satan has inundated us with sexual "choices," and chastity is not on his list. When it comes to the subject of sexuality, young people today are given incomplete choices. For example, assume that a math test had the problem, ten times ten equals x. You are given five multiple choices and you must choose an answer for x, but none of the five choices are correct. What would you be forced to do? You would be forced to choose something incorrect. *In the matter of sexuality, chastity is the right answer, but it is not on Satan's list of choices.* Even virginity would not be the right answer, because virginity is assumed for one who has committed to chastity. But, one can choose to live in chastity even after virginity has been lost.

Gender Identity Disorder is not orientation. Gender Dysphoria or Childhood Gender Nonconformity (CGN) is a condition in which children and teens do not conform to expected societal behavior. Some signs and traits of this condition include:

- Cross gender clothing and grooming preferences.
- Recreation that requires aloneness.

- Identification with characters of the opposite sex in stories, cartoons or films.
- Strong verbal confrontation without cause coupled with confusion.

Typical among those who are diagnosed includes a fascination with the clothing of the opposite sex. Even though this sometimes leads to a desire for cross dressing, it is well reported that over 75% of these individuals identify themselves as "heterosexual."

Among the many major studies in this area, Gender Dysphoria is accepted by many professionals to be both physiological and psychological. Medical research also indicates that gender nonconforming behaviors are relatively treatable such as testosterone deficiency or Congenital Adrenal Hyperplasia.

These are real-world issues that are prevalent in our society today. You may recall a male celebrity athlete announcing to the world that he felt like he was truly a female. How did you respond? Many Christians voiced their opinions about his confession in a rather questionable manner. Our actions sometimes speak louder than our words. I once witnessed a young wife prepare a good meal for her husband and then get so mad at him that she dumped it on the floor. She communicated her true feelings with her actions. Christians often react in the same manner. We forget that how we communicate can be just as important as what we are trying to communicate.

People that suffer with transgender related issues should not be maligned or mocked—we should love them and pray for them. Our response to them should be no different than it is for a dangerously thin person that is suffering from anorexia. Such a person may look in the mirror and see an overweight person. As a Christian, I wouldn't confront someone diagnosed with anorexia and say, "You are evil" or "Just get over it." That would be incredibly ignorant and insensitive. It would be equally wrong for me to enable that person by agreeing with them that they are overweight. Therefore, as a Christian, I must not enable a person that is suffering with a transgender disorder by agreeing with them, but neither will I scorn them for being unhealthy.

Johns Hopkins' former psychiatrist-in-chief, Dr. Paul McHugh, states that a sex change is "biologically impossible," and those who feel they are transgender are suffering from a "disorder of assumption." He also reported that the suicide rate among those who have had reassignment surgery is 20 times higher than people who have never struggled with "assumption disorder." Let's remember that God is not the author of confusion and that we wrestle not against flesh and blood. We are in a spiritual war—a war that grace always wins.

We are also, on occasion, asked about hermaphroditism, the medical term for those believed to have been born with both sexes. The simple answer is this: there is no such person as a true hermaphrodite. Regardless of tabloid rumor, there has never been a case in which both types of gonadal tissue function—ever. External genitalia in some cases are ambiguous, depending on the health of a person's chromosomes. In this case, a person should discover medically what gender they are according to their chromosomes and live accordingly.

Any thought you allow to be entertained can become a fantasy or desire. This can happen with any man involved in pornography. As he entertains the new thoughts and images put before him, he begins to desire things he once never desired. In the same way, Satan has legitimized sexual same sex attraction at every point. He has successfully distorted the truth in this world, and people now consider right as wrong and wrong as right. Hey, if it feels good, do it. A young person who has feelings of being alone and left out can now see this as a way to suddenly be accepted and even to become popular among his or her peers.

Appetites are no excuse for choices. Now, let us assume that the same sex attraction has become sexualized. This appetite still does not justify the choice to indulge. No doubt there are young men whose minds have indulged and who now fantasize about gay sex. Any person can develop an appetite for many things, either natural or unnatural. Nevertheless, having a desire for something does not make that thing acceptable in God's eyes. *It is still wrong to lose one's chastity at the altar of appetites (Ephesians 5:3; 1 Thessalonians 4:7).*

Retrospect often distorts reality. You have probably heard the saying that perception is ninety percent of reality. This is when reality becomes what you interpret it to be, not necessarily what it is. There may be times when a young person is asked leading questions such as, "Do you remember as a child having a longing to have a physical relationship with other boys?" In the courtroom, that would be considered a leading question. The answer is "yes" for every person, but to the confused young person, this leads them to a ridiculous conclusion.

3. Emotional same sex attraction. I save this one for last because this comes into play even before sexual same sex attraction. It can come into play after sexual same sex attraction, but in different ways.

My desire for emotional *same sex closeness* began when I was young and remains in place to this day. Men develop strong emotional ties with other men throughout their lives, and in fact, they even grow stronger over the years. The same is true with girls and women. Women are actually more comfortable with these feelings than men, but given the right stimulus, men can be demonstrative as well. Have you ever seen men on a sports team after winning a championship? Have you ever seen how men react in combat after a particularly difficult battle?

We bond emotionally with others of our sex in many different ways throughout our lives, and these bonds are often stronger than those among a husband and wife. The hugging of a group of men after winning the World's Series is not sexual. The hugging of two soldiers at the grave of their fallen comrade can be intense, but it is in no way sexual. The Bible says that Jonathan's love for David exceeded the love of a man for a woman. John had an emotional attraction to Jesus that was in no way sexual. Just consider this fact: no earthly relationship is carried into Heaven EXCEPT friendship. The marital, parental, and sibling relationships will not exist; only "friendship" will be transferable into Glory. This leads me to believe that it would be wise for us to strengthen the bonds of friendship within all our relationships.

There are some cultures in this world where men are not at all uncomfortable with physical (nonsexual) affection being displayed with other men. We are all, to some degree, a product of our environment and life experiences. The culture of the surrounding society or even within the family unit may cause some men to react or respond differently than we might expect.

Unfortunately, Satan never misses an opportunity to pervert pure affection by attaching innuendos of sexuality to them. In some cultures, boys are afraid to show their emotions towards other boys for fear of being teased or accused of being "gay." Same sex affection is not even close to being gay and, in fact, is most often pure. When a person feels these emotions towards another person, they should not be shamed or made to feel they are not normal. This is true with men and women, although society has accepted such affection between women more readily.

Two eunuchs of the same sex can develop a wonderful and chaste relationship with one another that is in *no way* sexual or romantic. They can have a bond that allows them to feel comfortable showing nonsexual affection, such as that which John showed to Jesus. By the way, it is interesting that although Jesus was a MAN, He accepted the affection of John without rebuke or refusal. Two eunuch men or women can live together in chastity as long as they remain mentally pure and avoid any appearance of evil.

Above Reproach

Now we come to a subject that can be difficult. When a man, woman, boy, or girl has developed same sex attraction in a sexual manner, is their right to emotional same sex closeness forfeited? The answer is no, but with exceptions. They have not forfeited that right, but they have created the responsibility of living above reproach.

Let me give you an illustration. A man who has struggled with lust and has a reputation for being a fornicator with women would likewise have a responsibility to avoid, not only the appearance of evil, but to abstain from that which could lead him into temptation. He should be careful about

58

where he goes and what he looks at. He must protect his mind. What if someone saw him hanging out in an area known for having heavy prostitution, but in truth he was actually soul winning? That could be wrong for him. Not only is he putting himself in a vulnerable position, but he is also creating an appearance of evil.

In regards to the eunuch, the same is true. You must not put yourself in temptation's way, nor should you be careless with the appearances that could make others question your activities. You can develop strong emotional same sex ties, but it may not be wise to share a living place or to show open affection too often towards one another.

Recognize your God-created need for intimacy and separate that from all things sexual. Repent or change the direction of your mind toward carnal choices. Same sex closeness is not same sex sexual attraction. Receive proper counsel and direction in areas of curiosity. Remember, today is tomorrow's memory. Do not waste today or give it away. You were born and given life for HIS purpose. Use your life for the Kingdom.

Chapter Six
CONFUSION AND DESPAIR

When it became apparent to Sam that he was not "normal," he was driven to a point of despair. Despair is the root word for desperation, which is what happens to many people like Sam. In their despair, they act out of desperation. Sam's despair drove him to contemplate suicide. This was a gifted and caring young man. He loved the Lord, his family, his church, and life itself. However, facing all of these things and believing that he may be "gay" was nearly more than he could bear.

It is always tragic when a life is lost or wasted, but I cannot help but wonder how many have been lost in this same type of scenario. It numbers in the tens of thousands, although there is no exact data to support my belief. We lose some to a lifestyle that is not the solution to their problem, and we lose some of them to suicide. Whenever that happens, there are tragic consequences.

- A precious life is lost.
- Scandal enters the church and family.
- Others are tempted, even empowered to do the same.

Sam is not alone. The message of this chapter should break the heart of everyone. The stories of lost lives are countless. We could begin with those who fought to find some normalcy in the "straight" world, only to give up and enter the "gay" lifestyle. Many young people who have grown up in Bible-believing churches under the teaching of the Scriptures are now completely away from the Lord, as well as the church. Some have tried to re-enter the church by pressuring us to divert our beliefs from the scriptural mandate. While I do not believe that we are instructed to shun these individuals, I do believe that we are to call it sin.

My heart is tender towards these helpless lost, because the conflict of their faith and their feelings often forces them to such despair that they did not want to go on living. Rather than bring a reproach to their families, their church, or their Savior, they gave up on life and decided that ending their life was their only viable alternative. I pay special tribute to them because their reason for ending their lives, while certainly flawed, still possessed a sense of nobility. They had become convinced that they were not "normal;" therefore, they *automatically* conclude they must be "gay." No one was there to show them the truth to set them free. Rather than stepping over a line into a lifestyle they believed was wrong, they stepped over another line, to end their agony and their life. I do not believe that these examples are rare.

These are stories of talented, loving, gifted, hopeful men and women who once saw their futures with hope and excitement. Lives were destroyed, because they did not understand why they did not have the same desires as other people.

People such as:

- Robert Hall, who, on June 15th, 2012, at the age of 15 took his own life. Robert did not feel an attraction to girls, and as a result, was subjected to bullying at his high school for not being a *normal* guy.
- John Wallace, a high school student in Pennsylvania, who committed suicide in 1997 because of constant harassment over his non-attraction to the opposite sex.
- Brandy Bryant, who, at the age of 27 took her own life by a self-inflicted gunshot wound. She had spent many years struggling with her non-attraction to the opposite sex.
- Timothy Clarkston, who in September 2010, at the age of 18, left his dorm room one evening to get something to eat. Instead, he made his way to the City Bridge and posted this message on Facebook from his cell phone: "jumping off the bridge sorry." He then jumped to his death. Tim had been tortured by his non-attraction to the opposite sex.

62

- Brandon Forks, of Indiana, had been bullied and tortured for his non-attraction toward the opposite sex. At the age of 15, he hanged himself from the rafters of his family's barn.
- Sean Carter, a 13 year old from California, was bullied and tortured for his non-attraction toward the opposite sex. He finally had taken all he could stand and hanged himself from a tree in his yard.
- Adam Baxley, of Houston, Texas, had been bullied and tortured for his non-attraction toward the opposite sex. He shot himself in the head when he was 13 years old.

Our Failure

The list could go on and on. It is sad...tragic. Why did it have to happen? It was because they had no answers to their dilemma. They did not desire death. It was not what they wanted, but it was the only way out that made sense to them. They did not have an answer for how they felt or what they were experiencing. You may say, "It was not because of their feelings they took their lives, but rather it was how people treated them." That is true to a certain extent, but not completely. These kids and this young woman could have dealt with the ridicule if they would have known what Sam learned. Like Sam, they were created in a special way and for a special purpose—to be natural-born eunuchs. People can accept suffering if they understand that there is a reason and have some outlet that helps them deal with their special circumstances. Unfortunately, they had no understanding of the truth and their despair led them to do something desperate.

Can you see where the church has failed these people? We have been a dark-house rather than a lighthouse. We have preached against their lack of desire towards the opposite sex rather than providing a scriptural answer for them. We have established a mold that has no place for their uniqueness. In some ways, we are as guilty as the ones who bullied them. We bullied them with our rhetoric and gave them no answer. If Christ is the answer, then why was there no answer for them? Were they supposed to pretend or fake feelings they did not have? Were they supposed to live a lie? What else were they to do, other than mistakenly decide they were "gay"? *What else, except take their life?*

There have been some high profile men in Christian circles whose children took their lives, and the rumors began circulating that perhaps they had been secretly gay. After hearing the description of these individuals, I am convinced they were not gay. They were probably eunuchs without understanding, without the truth.

William Penn once said, "O Lord, help me not to despise or oppose what I do not understand."

Novelist Dan Brown said, "We all fear what we do not understand."

This is true regarding these young people and most churches. We fear what we do not understand. We have not understood why a young man or a young woman is not attracted to someone of the opposite sex. In truth, we just do not understand what the Bible teaches. As a result, our misunderstanding has led to some terrible attributes in the church.

- *No sympathy.* How can we sympathize with something we assume is related to a sin rather than a calling? I was somewhat sympathetic before I became involved in this ministry, but nothing like I am today. After meeting and dealing with these individuals, I have come to love them for their uniqueness and to feel a deep compassion for them.
- *No solution.* I wonder how many times we have asked the Lord to give us an answer for these people. I am not special. I am not some super Christian to whom God gave a "special" revelation. I am a normal, average preacher who, with a broken heart, sought, and has continued to seek, for answers for a huge segment of our population.
- *No salvation.* It saddens me to say this, but many whom I love and respect, would damn these individuals to hell for that which God brought into their lives. Some would say you cannot be saved and become a homosexual. Well, I have news for you; Sam

was *saved.* Sadly, some might even assume that one with no desire must be lost; otherwise, they would have "normal" desires.

- *No salvaging.* We have no salvage plan for those who have left the church as Sam did because we have bought the lie that God has given up on them. No, He has not! The church may have given up because we had no solution, but God has not, does not, and will not give up on them. It is my experience that there are scores of people who are involved in the gay lifestyle who are so confused they do not know what to do. They know that they are born again. They know they love the Lord, but they feel this distortion of truth is the way God made them. They are angry, bitter, and hurt because the church does not want them. Many of them could be salvaged if the church wanted them. Christ wants them, and so should we.

- *No second chances.* We have another chance to do what *should have* been done. We have another chance to do those things we can and should do today. It's impossible to go back in time and change the beginning of these tragedies, but we can help change their endings. We can add value to those lives that were prematurely quenched by reaching those whom we know may be suffering with the same inner struggles. We could begin shining light today on the truth of Matthew 19. We could choose today to have sympathy for those who are hurting. We could choose today to teach Christ's solution, which is identifying *who* we are in HIM. We could choose today as the day we begin letting Christ be the Judge of others' salvation. We aren't even jurors; we are children saved by GRACE.

You could choose today to be a special day—the day you begin helping salvage lives of hurting people. Today could change tomorrow and eternity, not only in the life of one who's contemplating escape through suicide, but for you, for all of us, who realize that life is only a vapor.

Chapter Seven
IDENTITY OF A EUNUCH

Sam was quick to embrace his new identity when we spoke that evening. It was easy for him to declare, "I am not gay. I am a eunuch," while seated in the privacy of the office. However, the next day brought with it new challenges for Sam. For example:

- How much should he tell people about his past?
- How should he explain his newfound identity?
- How should he "define" or explain himself to others?

These are questions that were difficult for me to grasp. For a long time, I thought a eunuch would embrace their calling openly and with great pride. I imagined that they would proclaim to everyone, "I am a eunuch." After all, this was a special calling God had chosen for them. It finally became apparent to me that, for several reasons, it was not all that easy.

There were many negative connotations surrounding the word, "eunuch." When people think of a eunuch, they almost always immediately think of castration.

There were many who would be uncomfortable around one whom they discovered had struggled with sexual identity.

Many Christian institutions would shun them and even expel them if they discovered they were not attracted to the opposite sex. The moment someone discovers you have no attraction for the opposite sex, antennas go up and they fear you may be "gay." In fact, one of the greatest fears a eunuch faces is being falsely accused as being "gay."

Some sincere family members would be offended if others knew of their loved one's true identity. It would be ideal if everyone celebrated your newfound identity, but this is not an ideal world. Almost every person who has discovered their identity as a eunuch has had one or more family members who struggled to accept it or to believe it.

This has led me to realize that the declaration made by Sam that night is not one that always translates well into real life. There are some major questions most eunuchs face after discovering their true identity.

1. How can a eunuch identify himself or herself? Do they tell people they are a eunuch, considering the assumptions people have about eunuchs? One of their greatest fears is that people will not understand. They can hardly introduce themselves by saying, "Oh, by the way, I am a eunuch." Most people would immediately have a negative reaction. In spite of the fact that it is a biblical term, they would deem it to be strange, even unnatural. Most eunuchs discover other ways to explain themselves. For example, some will explain that they have chosen to live a life of consecrated chastity. Others may say they have chosen to remain faithfully unmarried. While they did not choose to be born a eunuch, it is true that they can choose to be chaste.

Every eunuch must choose this for themselves. It cannot be thrust upon them by another. There are some who will proudly proclaim the fact that they are a eunuch; however, for most this is not comfortable. They instead must decide how to identify themselves in a way that is honest and helpful for others to accept them.

2. How does one explain this discovery to those they love? How does one explain this to parents, siblings, or others with whom they have an intimate relationship? Oddly enough, it is often those you feel would be least likely to accept this who are most accepting, and those we feel would embrace it are often the most resistant. For this reason, it must be handled with much thought, prayer and care.

- Do not rush out and tell everyone. Take it slow. Be patient.
- Be prepared for mixed reactions. Not everyone will have the same reaction. You will experience some extremes.
- Rehearse your explanation to make it as clear as possible.

- Do not become impatient with those who do not immediately accept your explanation.
- Do not receive their confusion as rejection. The worst thing you can do is assume they are rejecting you merely because they do not understand.
- Use layman's terms. Do not complicate it. Explain it as clearly as possible.
- Do not be defensive when some struggle to understand.
- Do not immediately tell them about your past. If you committed sexual sins, be cautious about telling others the extent.
- There are some to whom you should never tell of your past, because they will never be able to accept the truth.

Consider opening the dialogue with an email or a letter so that you are able to determine exactly what you want to say. When talking to someone in person, emotions will play into the conversation, and you may not be able to clearly and accurately communicate everything because of the emotions that you, and they, are experiencing. Some people may be able to better communicate this in person, but others may do better in writing.

3. How does one explain it to others in their daily walk? How do they tell their pastor or others who are out there trying to "set them up" with a date? What should they do when they fear the possibility of being compromised in a Christian school or college because the leadership does not understand the truth? Face it, we live in a society that promotes dating and marriage and not everyone is going to leave you alone when they discover the truth about you.

Now comes the part when you must begin to reveal your discovery to others. As mentioned before, do so with great compassion for those to whom you are explaining your situation. Do not feel they must understand immediately. Give them time, and let the Lord work on their hearts.

It may be temporary, but there will be rejection. If you think everyone will embrace the truth, you are deceiving yourself. To many, you are exposing a truth that is totally foreign to them. Be understanding of that fact. Let your testimony show them that you have truly committed your life to Christ in a special way. Over time, people will begin to accept the truth and, in doing so, will accept you.

4. How much does one reveal of their past sins? Do they reveal it to the entire church? Do they tell everyone what they have done? What if they were only mildly involved in homosexual behavior and they repented before it became known? Simply put, most people do not need to know. David said of his sins, *"Against thee and thee only have I sinned and done this evil in thy sight."* Most people are not capable of dealing with the details of your sins, nor are you obligated to tell them. Here are a few suggestions:

- Tell only those that need to know in order to guide and strengthen you. Sometimes that is not family.
- Do not tell the church as a whole. One day, God may lead you to tell your story, but until then, be careful.
- Do not go into details. You do not need to relive it, and they do not need to hear it.
- Expect some to react uncomfortably. Be prepared for this reaction and do not feel you must be defensive.

5. How does a eunuch help others while remaining discreet? This is not always for the sake of the eunuch, but for those close to him or her who are still uncomfortable with the truth. The old statement, "Discretion is the better part of valor," is certainly applicable in this situation. What should one do when they feel there is someone who may be struggling with the same issues? First, and foremost, do not come on too strong. Be an encouragement to them and look for opportunities to introduce your testimony to them. Do not just blurt it out. Start slowly and feel out the situation to see if there are signs they are relating to your message. Nothing helps one struggling person like the transparent confession of another who has struggled with the exact same issues.

Sometimes, you may want to begin by sharing small amounts of information about your story to prepare them for the entirety of the truth.

Select parts of your story that you believe will most help that individual. Pray diligently before you approach them. Go to them in God's wisdom and not your own.

Most eunuchs are sensitive to signals from others who are in the same situation from whence they came or who are struggling with their identity. They see the signs and their heart is tender to the pain they remember. While they cannot automatically assume that others will be as receptive, they can begin to reach out and ask for the Lord to open the door for them to introduce the subject at the proper time.

Chapter Eight
FALLACY OF
SECULAR LABELS

Heterosexual?

I am not a heterosexual. This is often the first thing I tell a person when I meet with them regarding their sexual identity. Sam, and those like him, have often labeled themselves long before I ever meet with them. Sam, for example, had chosen to place upon himself the label of "gay" or "homosexual," not because it described what he wanted to be, but because it described what he was led to believe he was.

At the time I first met with Sam, I was under the belief that there were certain labels that described our sexuality. I would have at one time considered myself to be a heterosexual male. I would have considered someone such as Sam, before I met him, to be a homosexual. But as I have dealt with this issue and those who have become involved in it, I have become aware of the fallacy of these and other labels.

Where Did These Labels Originate?

The terms homosexual and heterosexual originated in 1869 when they were coined by a man named Karl Kertbeny, a man terribly confused about human sexuality. In fact, his confusion and depravity was so severe, that it effectively impaired his moral judgment and general decency. Kertbeny even attempted to normalize bestiality (sex with animals), coining the term "heterogenits."

So the same person who invented a label for "heterosexuals," also invented the terms for other sexual deviations. He did so with a desire to legitimize unnatural sexual behavior. Karl later changed his name to Maria and died at age 58.

Satan Labels Mankind

Adam and Eve lost Paradise because the Serpent deceived them into believing they could be "gods." By using fear, Satan caused the Hebrew people to see themselves as "grasshoppers" next to their enemy. As a result, they were left to wander in the wilderness for 40 years. Jonathan's son, Prince Mephibosheth, had been deceived into labeling himself as nothing more than a "dog" until King David adopted him. On one occasion, Jesus healed an unnamed demon possessed man, but when asked, the man "demonically" said, "I am Legion." How sad for Christians to fall into the trap of secular and, in some cases, even demonic labels. Labeling someone "homosexual" and "heterosexual" is disgraceful, anti-biblical, and destructive.

God's Labels Are Always Best

God labels sexual behavior: natural or unnatural. I have heard some Christians, attempting to sound bold, use terms such as "homo," "queer," and even "faggot" to label those who are sexually deviant. We run into several biblical issues when we use these derogatory names, but let's consider a couple.

The use of these labels does not communicate the love of Christ. I have had Christians defend their "sharp tongue" by reminding me that Jesus called the Pharisees such things as "snakes" and "scorpions." My reply? Jesus also walked on water, how about you? Why aren't you a water-walker yet? Maybe because Jesus didn't *command* you to walk on water. Part of "rightly dividing" the Word of God means that we must understand the difference between what Jesus did and what He commanded us to do. For example, Jesus fasted 40 days in seclusion, but He never once commanded us to do the same. Jesus, as both God and the Son of Man, did many mighty works. It is true that sometimes He chastised the Pharisees, but He commanded us to "love them" and "do them good."

Another reason we shouldn't use these terms and labels is simple. **They do not help anyone**. For the most part, our culture owns these labels and in some cases wearing them has become a badge of honor. A man living in sexual sin may very well identify himself as "queer" or "gay." They

74

have taken pride in some of these labels. These labels do not "convict" anyone either, as if that were our job anyway. God's terminology however is powerful. His Word always cuts to the heart. A man might convince himself to take pride in the "gay" label, but he won't take pride in the term "unnatural."

Why This Is So Important?

It is important because once we accept the term "homosexual" as a definition, we are legitimizing that a person can *be* a homosexual, that he could be born that way, that God made him a homosexual, that he has no choice in the matter, or that he is NOT a "heterosexual." The Bible never makes such a claim.

In Scripture, God created a man and a woman who then bore children who were men and women. These men and women are capable of homosexual acts, but God never says that a person *is* a homosexual. Even the word "sodomite" is a description of a person who chooses to perform perverted sexual behavior with someone of the same sex in exchange for something of value, but a person, by definition, is not inherently a sodomite. Sodomy is an act, not a title.

Why would we accept the terms "heterosexual" and "homosexual" after learning of their origin? Even when we use the term "heterosexual," we automatically acknowledge the idea that someone can be a "homosexual." By accepting these terms in our vocabulary, we have lost the right foundation. Our efforts are very much like trying to nail jelly to a tree—an exercise in futility.

God created men and women—not homosexuals and heterosexuals. In fact, God does not give any sexual orientation labels in the Bible. So, why do we?

Some Possible Reasons

We think we need to identify our orientation. If there are variations, then we need to identify ours. *Actually there are no variations, just deviations.* A deviation is an action that departs from an established course or accepted

75

standard. By accepting the label of heterosexual, we make the deviation into a variation.

We want to separate ourselves from those who choose unnatural lifestyles. In attempting to distance ourselves from the idea of being one thing, we legitimize it. I am very comfortable not identifying myself as a heterosexual because I am not trying to identify myself as such. God created me and calls me a man. My affections are natural. I do not need to label that, just live it.

Satan has deceived our culture into thinking these labels are legitimate. Once again, understanding who and why these names were conceived should be enough to nullify their use. The *origin* of these terms should provoke you to forsake these labels altogether. Why should we allow any man to redefine what God has already made clear? We are human-beings—not human-doings.

It appears to give clarity when, in truth, it only adds to the confusion. When there is a socially acceptable name for the behavior that deviates from God's plan, then we create more confusion by validating it.

So, Who Are You, Really?

We live in a culture of pride—a nation consumed with self. In this Age of Self, the language is filled with phrases that glorify mankind instead of God. Pride elevates personal choice above all other values: self-determination, self-knowledge, self-esteem, self-help, and even do-it-yourself. The touchstone of belief today is the individual, not his Maker. In this climate, Christians should accept no secular terms without scrutiny.

Who Has the Right to Label You?

We often are unsure about who we are because our society becomes our point of reference. We allow others to dictate to us how we perceive ourselves and then make their perceptions of us our own. We are often measured and judged by others–either as acceptable or unacceptable–and we allow our performance to define us. The truth is: neither we nor society have the right to label ourselves or others.

Would you allow a stranger to walk in your home and place his name over all of your belongings? Of course you wouldn't. No one has the right to label or re-label what belongs to you. There are only three situations that give us or anyone the right to label something.

- **Did I create it?** If I created it, then I can label it.
- **Do I own it?** If I own something, it is mine to label.
- **Did I purchase it?** If I bought it, then I have the right to name it whatever I like.

God is the only reliable source of our true identity. He created us, loves us, sent His Son, Jesus Christ, to die for us, and He transforms our lives through His Holy Spirit. *"For ye are bought with a price: therefore, glorify God in your body, and in your spirit, which are God's"* (1 Corinthians 6:20).

When we allow Him to define our identity, we stand on a sure foundation for a life of peace, contentment, and yes, even some adventure. When we establish our identity in how God sees us, we can confidently live our lives in the assurance of His perfect plan for our lives.

Until we discover that perfect identity God made for us, we are left to be cheapened by mere sexual identities coined by man. It is sad when a man limits his identity to something temporary when God offers an identity that is eternal.

A New Identity

The Bible tells us, *"Therefore if any man be in Christ, he is a new creature: old things are passed away; behold all things are become new"* (2 Corinthians 5:17). But what does it mean to be a "new creation"? It means we have a new identity. That NEW identity has amazing implications for how we live our lives and how God works in and through us.

John 1:12 – *But as many as received Him, to them gave He power to become the sons of God, even to them that believe on His name.*

Chapter Nine

HIDDEN TRUTHS

The Truth Hidden in Plain Sight

Before I met Sam, I would not have noticed anything unique about him. However, since we met, I have realized that there are young people like Sam all around me. They were always there, but they were hidden in plain sight. Perhaps I thought they were different, but now, I know they are special and that God made them the way they are. The same can be said about the truth found in Scripture regarding eunuchs. It has always been there, but Satan successfully distracted us from seeing it.

Most people are familiar with the FedEx logo. But, did you know that there is actually an arrow in their logo? In fact, it is in plain sight, yet there was a time when I did not know it was there. I saw the logo, but I did not see the arrow. You could say that it was *hidden in plain sight.* Still can't see it? Look between the E and the x and you will find it. If you had never seen it before, it is not because it was not there. It was. In fact, when the designers were creating the logo, they purposely put it there, yet many people never saw it until it was pointed out to them.

The same thing is true regarding the teachings about eunuchs. The Bible is filled with examples of faithfully unmarried people. Jesus explained it to us. It is not some secret, yet like the arrow in the FedEx logo, we could not see it until someone pointed it out to us. Jesus predicted this when He said, "All men cannot receive this saying, save they to whom it is given" (Matthew 19:11). The fact is that truth cannot make a person free until someone points it out to them. Many Christians are unaware of this truth because no one has pointed it out. However, once they see it, it becomes clear to them.

The Bible tells us that, when we know the truth, the truth will make us free. What then happens when the truth is hidden, even if in plain sight? Obviously, people are not made free, and if they are not made free, they are held in bondage. Right before our eyes, there are people who have been enslaved by fears, doubts and confusions about why they are different. This often leads to an even greater bondage of a life in an unnatural and sinful lifestyle. They cannot be made free without the truth. However, we cannot make them free if we have missed seeing the truth. Often, we cannot clearly see those who are right in front of us, because we do not know the truth. This leads us to miss signals in the lives of people that we otherwise might have seen if we knew the truth.

Missed Signals

We live in a world of signals. We have traffic signals, athletic signals, warning signals, and about every other kind of signal imaginable. In fact, in most walks of life, there are some types of signals. Some of these are clearly defined, while others are less obvious and can even be a little obscure. These signals serve as non-verbal communications that allow us to send and receive messages.

When I first met my wife, I began to look for signals. I wanted to see if she was interested in me. In every situation, people are sending or looking for signals. Some of these signals come from our subconscious. For example, what husband has not come home to find his wife behaving differently than normal only to discover later that he has missed some signal completely? We remind each other of things using signals. We attract others with signals. We even express our interest and feelings about others with signals.

At times, mixed signals can create minor problems that have no devastating long term effects. However, at other times, missed signals can cause a catastrophic tragedy that costs people their lives. That is why in most occupations, employees are taught to be aware of indicators. Policemen are carefully trained in identifying clues that could indicate that a person has committed or is about to commit a crime. Successful businesses are aware of the importance of picking up on certain signals, given intentionally or unintentionally by their clients and customers.

One key to a good relationship is perception. If we are perceptive, we often can read signals and deal with things appropriately. Sadly, many pastors, parents and spiritual leaders miss obvious signals that some in their care may be eunuchs from birth. Perhaps it is because we are ignorant of the entire concept, or perhaps it is because we find some discomfort in admitting or accepting the idea that these individuals are uniquely different. We may even create the obstacles that hinder our relationship. A parent may ignore the signals because of their strong desire for grandchildren. Tragically, these missed signals often lead to lives that are totally ruined and wasted.

We must maintain the proper perspective. Sometimes we need to be reminded. What is better? Is it better for a eunuch to live the life that God intended for His glory or should the eunuch live a life that we consider appropriate? God forbid that we ever cause someone not to live the life that God uniquely designed for that individual.

We cannot say that we did not see the signals, because after we hear of one of our own proclaiming that they are "gay," we hear something like, "I am not surprised. They were always different from the other kids." That tells me that the signals were there, but we either chose to ignore them or we did not know what to think of them. In dealing with those who were "born that way," I have learned to pick up on certain signals that indicate to me that a person may be a eunuch.

Eunuch Signals

What are the signals, mannerisms, interests, and associations that we should be looking for to identify these special people? Knowing these signals will help us minister to those under our care:

Is their disposition kind, affectionate, loving? Most eunuchs are sensitive individuals. That is not unusual for most women, but not always as prevalent in men. However, in many men who are born as a eunuch, these attributes may be more prevalent.

Do they yearn for same sex companionship? All men enjoy the company of other men, and relationships with eunuchs may be easily formed. However, other male relationships may be more difficult to establish.

Is he an anomaly with a combination of courage and timidity? The eunuchs I have met are, for the most part, courageous, but they also are a little insecure. They have the courage of masculinity, but the quietness of femininity.

Does he sometimes exhibit flamboyance? One characteristic many eunuchs have which is often seen in the so called "homosexual" lifestyle is a combination of quiet nobility and flamboyance. They like flashy colors and they enjoy the things that we may often equate with femininity.

Are they touchy/feely individuals? Men are not normally this way. If you watch a men's professional golf tournament, the men all shake hands when the match is concluded. Unless he is the one who wins the tournament, you will seldom see hugs. However, if you watch a ladies' professional golf tournament, you will often see them hug each other after the tournament is over. In general, women hug more than men; however, eunuchs are more prone to touch than other men.

Is he comfortable being associated with the company of girls/women? Eunuchs often feel comfortable in the company of women, more so than with men. Perhaps it is because they feel a bit intimidated by their differences. Many homosexual men have close, sisterly-like relationships with other women. Guys like to hang out with guys, but eunuchs prefer the company of women.

Is his appearance important to him? Does he desire to be seen as "lovely"? Does he like to wear bright clothing and colors that are more often associated with women? A eunuch may be extremely fashion conscious. Physical appearance is extremely important to them.

82

Is there a need to care for others? Women are by nature usually more nurturing than men. However, you will discover that male eunuchs possess that same nurturing quality. They are tender and loving. They are predisposed to being protective and caring for others.

Does he easily complement an alpha-male in a project or ministry? Many male eunuchs work well as the counterpart to alpha-males because they enjoy supplementing success rather than originating it. They are less competitive or ego-driven than other men. Perhaps it would be wise to pair eunuchs with an alpha-male in a ministry.

Does he enjoy it when people pay attention to him? Eunuchs are happy if they are made to feel important or special. They thrive on this attention. They do not need to be the hero, but they do want to feel they have a special place with the one they are serving. The born-eunuch's natural temperament is one that could easily lead him to jealousy or conceit. Is he indeed a modern day "son of thunder" who needs to have a special place?

This is not intended to be a stereotype of eunuchs. However, these are characteristics that many eunuchs possess. Tragically, we have placed everyone into our own mental mold, and we often fail to recognize the uniqueness of these individuals. We need to identify these special individuals and guide them into finding God's will for their lives. How we respond could have a life-altering effect on their lives, so let's establish some principles with regard to these signals.

Common Mistakes

Do not jump to conclusions. Most car wrecks are tragedies that could have been easily prevented had the driver not reacted in fear by "over-correcting." For example, if a small cat or dog dashes in front of the car, rather than applying the brakes properly or moving slightly to the left or right, we over-correct—jerk the wheel and crash. This could certainly be a temptation for those who have loved ones that may display some of the prosaic signals listed above. Do not jump to conclusions; proceed with caution. Here are some ways people over-correct:

83

Trying to "toughen up" a young boy by pressuring him to participate in sports or expecting him to enjoy them. A child believes many things because mom or dad "say it's so," but our actions can be like a megaphone to children. Do not try to define masculinity or femininity to your child by trying to make them something they are not. This only sets them up for failure by creating an expectation they may never meet.

Attempting to create an attraction for the opposite sex by stimulating or over emphasizing sexual behavior. For example, a dad may say to his son, "Check out her curves! Wouldn't you like a girl with curves like that?" This is a *dangerous* move on the part of a parent because it opposes the teaching of chastity and makes sexual attraction an issue.

Disconnecting with the child. Perhaps we are so put out and disappointed in their behaviors that we actually disconnect with them. What that tells the child is this: you love them if they act "acceptably," but not if they do not. Do not treat them any different. Apathy should be avoided at any cost. A proactive parent does not have to over-correct or redefine anything; all they *must* do is parent. Parenting is like shepherding in a lot of ways, but one way in particular is this: sheep are led, not driven. Lead your children by example. Show them that, no matter what, the main business in life is to love Jesus and follow Him.

Criticizing their personality. When a child feels he cannot please his parent, he will seek others he can please. Making critical remarks is the wrong reaction. Innuendo and supposition will only strain a relationship. Remember, it is often the *negative treatment* toward one who has fallen which does more damage than the individual's actual fall.

Suggestions

Promote scriptural principles. The world tells us to keep an "open mind." The Christian must keep a spiritual mind. We do that by openly and properly teaching passages such as Matthew 19, thus rightly dividing the Word of Truth. Use the Bible to teach, not only the valor of a man like David who fought Goliath, but also the tenderness of David who dearly loved Jonathan.

Biblical education is fundamental for children to possess a correct view of themselves in light of God and His Word. It is especially important in deciphering their personal uniqueness and learning how God specially created them. They must come to realize that God makes no mistakes, so they are not an accident or a mistake.

Teach them to have the right understanding of their own unique purpose. What is their purpose? It is to honor and glorify the Lord with their lives. It is *not* to discover their sexuality, but to discover their purpose for God and to serve Him in the best way possible.

Teach your children that personality does not shape sexuality. Humanism views sex and sexuality as simple acts or orientations developed as a byproduct of evolution. In evolution, the dysfunctional is always praised as the next mutant formation within the evolutionary process. This is why we have a myriad array of sexual orientations. Humanism begs you and your children to choose one of their definitions of sexuality. Whether it is homosexual, heterosexual, bisexual, pansexual, or polysexual, pick one and they will be happy. This is foolish. None of these terms are found within Scripture. They are simply unnatural and mythological.

The Bible says God created man and that He also created woman. There is no biblical truth of sex apart from one man and one woman. Any humanistic definition outside of Scripture is unnatural. This means it is not wise to subscribe to the humanistic labels of society within the home. Let the term homosexual be changed to the biblical term *"unnatural affection."* Try to steer away from all such labels, even including the term heterosexual. Again, use the biblical terms of <u>man</u> and <u>woman</u>.

Let your children know that you are proud of them, not only for the way they are made, but because of the way they let God use them. Understand this, certain signals, mannerisms, and interests, do not make the person, but they can influence who they become. The world wants to define us based upon our signals, actions, and what we do. God seeks to reveal who we are based on how He sees us. He wants to reveal to us what we were always created to be. These signals are a broad generalization of those who might have been born that way and should not be seen as indicative of all eunuchs. It is, however, a fair assessment that might help someone.

Chapter Ten
REASON IS NO EXCUSE

Expose the Truth, Remove the Excuse

In these past couple of years since I first met with Sam, I have seldom had to confront those who were living in the "gay" lifestyle with the fact of the sinfulness of their behavior. Sam knew it was a sin. However, he also felt that it was the only choice he had. That may sound like a contradiction, but it is not. Most people can find an excuse for the sinful choices they make. If, as many of these people assume, I was born this way, then I have no alternative but to make this choice. We know this is not true, but it is the rationale for most of the sins we all commit. The greatest hindrance to repentance is excuse.

In my meeting with Sam, I knew I had two basic challenges. First, I needed to expose the truth and then I needed to remove any excuses he might have. Both of these went hand in hand. I was not meeting with Sam to give him an excuse for his sin, nor was I there to condemn him in his sin. I was there to tell him the truth and let the truth make him free. What is the truth? First, it is that the lifestyle in which he was living was a sinful one and unacceptable to God. Secondly, it was to provide an escape from the confusion that led him to choose to partake of that sin. In doing this, I was removing his excuse and leading him to an escape.

Without Excuse

This is the challenge in dealing with anyone who has chosen to live in sin. They may have legitimate reasons, but they are still without excuse. In Romans, we see Paul describing the awful condition in which the Romans were living, yet he made it clear that there was no excuse for any of their sinful behaviors.

Romans 1:20 – *For the invisible things of him from the creation of the world are clearly seen, being understood by the things that are made, even his eternal power and Godhead; so that they are without excuse.*

Human reasoning often excuses sins. We blame circumstances, individuals, difficulties, even God for the choices we make, but God makes it very clear that these excuses do not excuse us. In dealing with eunuchs who have entered into the sins of unnatural affection, the challenge is seldom that they do not know in their hearts that what they are doing is sinful. After all, the Bible says it is unnatural behavior. Even some who were unsaved when I first met them admitted that they knew that they were engaging in an unacceptable (unnatural) behavior.

While I do not deny that there were legitimate reasons for the choices Sam made, I could not allow those reasons to be excuses that would block his repentance and subsequent restoration. There are a number of reasons that so many who are born to be eunuchs end up in the sins they do.

Before dealing with the reasons given, I must make it clear that not every person who engages in unnatural behavior was born to be a eunuch. Most of those with whom I have met have been born eunuchs, but there are those who merely have allowed their lusts to consume them and lead them into these sinful activities. Make no mistake about it; Satan desires to lead as many as he can into these unnatural sins using any means possible.

Now that we have clarified that point, allow me to offer several reasons/excuses that are often used which do not stand up to scrutiny.

1. Churches and Christians have mishandled the truth. Many living in this unnatural lifestyle have used the excuse that Christians have condemned them. They love to justify themselves by pointing out that God is love. Of course what we call love is often a total mischaracterization of God's love. Somehow they feel that this puts the responsibility on churches and Christians to accept them in their sin and, in some cases, even to condone it. After all, their excuse is that God made them this way. My reply is, as Paul said in Galatians 4:16, *"Am I therefore become your enemy, because I tell you the truth?"* If I tell you the truth in the wrong way, I have still told you the truth. My motive, my method, and my spirit do not change the fact that truth is still truth.

The challenge for many who have turned to the unnatural lifestyle is that they see one of two options. If they accept that succumbing to their "same sex" attraction is a sin, then they often face the idea that their particular sin is one that is unforgivable in the eyes of many Christians. Therefore, they are left to justify (or excuse) their sin on the misinterpretation of Scripture or the hatefulness of Christians. That is what has led to the ludicrous debate as to whether same sex marriage should be condoned by churches, somehow thinking that if we are not going to condemn them, then we must condone them. That leaves these individuals captive to their sinful lifestyle. My job is to tell the truth and let the truth make them free, not to justify, excuse, or ignore the sin, but to provide hope, which can only be found in Christ. It is a hope that in Him they can live without giving in to the sin and have a purpose in Jesus Christ our Savior.

In many cases, churches and Christians have mistreated those living in unnatural lifestyles. I find myself caught right in the middle on this particular claim. While I recognize that there has been some hateful rhetoric spewed at those engaged in this sin with little hope given, I cannot allow this to be an excuse for those who choose to enter into this unnatural lifestyle. Mistreatment is no excuse for sin. If it was, then all of us could excuse ourselves for some sin in our lives. I wish the name calling and hatefulness did not exist, but again I must remind you that the truth will make you free and that means free from the bitterness of this mistreatment. Jesus was innocent, yet He was mistreated by the religious leaders of His day. He never once used it as an excuse. He was tempted in all points as are we, yet without sin (Hebrews 4:15).

2. I was born with no sexual attraction to the opposite sex. That is not an acceptable excuse, because it does not give you the right to pursue *unnatural* attractions. This excuse of having been born with no attraction to the opposite sex has often been used as a reason, but with no apparent explanation. In Matthew 19, Jesus gives us the explanation for people who are born without these desires. Unfortunately, the explanation has been ignored, and there are some Christians who will always find a reason to debate Jesus' words. Some eunuchs are faced with this when they try to explain to family or friends their newfound discovery. They are confronted with doubts and debate, because it appears to be a new truth.

May I say to those who have used this as their excuse: when you know the truth, it will make you free not only of the sin, but of the excuse for the sin. It is amazing to see the peace in the lives of eunuchs who at one time chose the unnatural lifestyle, but have been set free with the truth.

Do not misunderstand me, we as Christians are responsible to represent truth in the right fashion. Whether we do or don't, it does not change the truth of God, nor does it give anyone an excuse for ignoring God's truth.

3. Jesus never spoke of it as being a sin. This is one reason/excuse that is being used to justify the unnatural lifestyle even by some churches and Christians. It saddens me that rather than finding freedom in truth, some remain in their bondage by this most flimsy excuse. Please understand that *every Word of God is Jesus*, not merely those He spoke with His own lips. John teaches us: *"And the Word was made flesh, and dwelt among us"* (John 1:14). Jesus came to fulfill the Law, not negate it, which means that every Word of God is still true. All teaching about unnatural behavior is still true, even if the manner in which we address it has been changed through the finished work of Christ. Let it be clear; the wages of sin is *still* death and sin when it is finished *still* brings death (Romans 6:23; James 1:15). Jesus did not come to put His stamp of approval on any sin. Some ordinances and practices He abolished, but sin is still sin.

4. I have a desire for the same sex. If that is true, it is not an acceptable excuse. That is called lust. Lust is never an excuse for us to sin. A man who lusts for a woman who is not his wife is not excused to act upon that lust. I have oft heard it said, "If God did not want me to participate in these activities, why did He give me these desires?" Be careful, my friend. God never tempts us to sin. That is like a young man saying, "If God did not want me to have sexual relationships with other women, why did he give me this lust?" or a pedophile saying, "If God did not want me to have sex with children, why did he give me this attraction to children?"

90

James said, *"Let no man say when he is tempted, I am tempted of God: for God cannot be tempted with evil, neither tempteth he any man: But every man is tempted, when he is drawn away of his own lust, and enticed"* (James 1:13, 14). There are two important truths here. First, God never tempts any man to do evil. Secondly, when we are tempted, it is because we are drawn by our own unique lusts. James says that we are all tempted by being drawn into our own lusts. If you lust for something natural or unnatural, that is not of God. There is no excuse. Lust is not an excuse. It is a cause for sin. I have natural attraction for the opposite sex, but it is my responsibility not to allow my attraction to turn into lust, lest I be drawn away by my lusts into fornication or adultery. Even if you feel an attraction to the same sex, it is no excuse for allowing it to become a lust for unnatural behavior.

Again, lust is no excuse to sin. Our knowledge of right and wrong may determine how much sin is imputed to us, but at the end of the day, no competent person has an excuse to sin—even the unsaved. Like any other sin, unholy sexual behavior—of any kind—must be dealt with in the same manner as we would deal with lying, cheating, or thievery. All sexual sin, regardless of its color or shape, is a result of lust. When it comes to sexual activity, there is only one benchmark by which to measure right or wrong, and that is the Word of God—not man's opinion.

What if, because of sin and its curse, a person *is* born with a disposition toward same-sex attraction? That would still not excuse the choice to sin. Temptation does not control a man. It has no power except that which we give it. If we feed our self-seeking nature only that which pleases it, we are choosing to sin. This has nothing whatsoever to do with a particular disposition. All of us have dispositions that lend themselves to certain sins. Ultimately, we all must make the choice whether to sin or not.

5. I was not raised in the right environment or I was molested as a child.
I will tread very carefully over this subject. There are those who are living in the unnatural lifestyle who have expressed the fact that they were molested or abused as a child. I have no doubt as to the validity of this point. My heart bleeds for these individuals. However, abuse or molestation may be your reason, but it is still no excuse. My friend, the

truth can still make you free. There are those who have turned to drugs or alcohol as a result of such mistreatment. There are others who have turned to prostitution or other sexual sins. There are even those who have become violent abusers as a reaction to how they themselves were mistreated. While I do not want to appear insensitive in any way, I must speak the truth in love. You have no excuse for your choices. No doubt, psychology and sociology have provided legitimate insight into the whys and wherefores of sinning. Yet there is a problem with this line of reasoning: explanation too often becomes exoneration. There is no excuse, even if we understand what motivates a person's actions. *Predictable sin does not mean acceptable sin in God's eyes.*

In fact, the majority of victims from child abuse have natural relationships with the opposite sex once they are adults. So, we can't really reduce the overall cause to childhood abuse. We can say that abuse is a complication, and most would agree that it is a huge complication to a person's life.

Excusing sinful behavior as being a result of the environment, peer-pressure, or low self-image may be sophisticated and it may provide insight into the nature of a person or the defects in our society, but it is not an excuse for sin. Sin is always born from our knowledge of what is right, coupled with our choice to do wrong.

Some may be quick to say that "child abuse" is the main factor in driving someone to unnatural sexual persuasions, and negative parent/child relationships are also common arguments used for the cause of unholy sexual behavior. Nevertheless, we have found that many who immerse themselves within the community of unnatural sexual activity actually have good parental relations, many even from good Christian homes.

There will always be some who say that these may have been factors, but the percentage is not higher than the rest of society. So, a negative relationship with a parent may be another complication, but it would be a fallacy to say it was the cause.

6. I was born "gay" due to my sin-nature. There are a plethora of birth defects people are born with every day: blindness, deafness, heart problems, and cancers are just a few examples. Is it possible then for someone to be born with a gay orientation?

Certainly, on the surface this argument appears logical—even scriptural, but close examination exposes this thought as a gross error and a dangerously flawed theory.

There have been a few scientists that were confident they would find an actual "gay gene," but it turned out to be much more complicated—they found nothing.

In fact, science revealed the "born gay" hypothesis to be utterly untrue. Studies using identical twins identified several cases where one sibling identified as straight while the other as gay. These studies are significant—sexual confusion is not biological, but spiritual in orientation.

People are complicated and that is for sure. It's hard to resolve our own confusion at times, much less understand what is happening inside another person's mind. However, if it takes a "sinful nature" to sin, then are we saying that Adam and Eve were created with a sinful nature? After all, Adam and Eve *did* sin.

I contend that just because something isn't genetic doesn't mean it's voluntary. My first language is English and that is not genetic, but it wasn't a voluntary choice, at least not by me. Why would I not learn to speak English? My English language is a product of my culture. Spiritually, we are not born *with* sin, but we are born into a world of sin; a culture that is disconnected from God.

God calls babies "holy" and even says that we should become like little children. Our flesh, even from birth, is not full of sin, but it is a perfect sponge for sin. It's not what we are born *with* that we call a "sin nature" it's what we're born *without*. Paul said, "I know that in me (that is, in my flesh,) dwells no good thing" (Romans 7:18). In Hosea 4:6, God says, "My people are destroyed for lack of knowledge." Voids create a vacuum that we often fill with sin. It is only through Christ that our voids and the sin that fills them can be destroyed.

Therefore, I can certainly understand why some people cling to the "born gay" narrative, because they believe it justifies how they are meant to live. Hence, the difference between a physical defect and a spiritual void—physical deficiency is never sinful. Stumbling over an object is a behavioral result of blindness, yet a person born blind is not committing a sin by stumbling. Thus it is easier to excuse an action by claiming the action is a result of the way you were born. If a person is born gay in the same way someone is born blind, then same-sex fornication is merely the behavioral result of their birth and cannot be condemned. Scripture denies this: there is no excuse for sin. Fornication, as with every sin, is the result of a spiritual void which must be destroyed.

In Conclusion

God is very clear that there are no excuses that will justify sin. However, there are often reasons for the choices we make. According to Romans 1:18-21, God's anger is revealed against all sin, making each and every human being without excuse when we ultimately face Him—even if the only light a person has is that of God's creation. No one will be able to face God and say, "How was I supposed to know that I was a sinner?" No, every person on this planet has some knowledge of their depraved spiritual state. They may be trying to delude themselves and others, but there is a certain level of knowledge that is implicit.

Moses is a good example of one who made a choice not to make excuses even in light of potential reasons. How did he do it? Notice the pattern in the following passage.

Hebrews 11:24-26 – *By faith Moses, when he was come to years, refused to be called the son of Pharaoh's daughter; Choosing rather to suffer affliction with the people of God, than to enjoy the pleasures of sin for a season; Esteeming the reproach of Christ greater riches than the treasures in Egypt: for he had respect unto the recompense of the reward.*

- He refused to be labeled.
- He chose to suffer rather than compromise.
- He took his self-esteem from Christ.

94

- He respected the consequences of wrong and the reward for right.

That is exactly what a person living in the unnatural lifestyle must do. There is no excuse for anyone to continue in their sin, no matter how good a reason they think they may have. The choice is yours.

Chapter Eleven
FEMALE EUNUCHS

Born That Way

When I first began working with Sam, my mindset was geared mostly towards young men like Sam. For the most part, I assumed that eunuchs were men. I knew that many women in history took vows of chastity and celibacy, but I never considered the idea that there were women "born that way" too. However, it was not long before several women approached me to let me know that they, too, were born without an attraction for men. Upon closer study of the Scriptures, I came to realize that nowhere was it said that born eunuchs were only men.

History is filled with examples of women who were made eunuchs by the works of men or who chose to be eunuchs by faith. However, the more I studied this idea, the more evidence I found that throughout Christian history there have been many women who were chosen by God to be eunuchs. The idea that all men and women were always meant to marry has stifled this out of churches, but many women have been as confused as men by their lack of attraction to the opposite sex.

In Matthew 19, where Jesus is teaching on eunuchs, we find something quite unusual. As we saw in chapter 4, if we study the original language, we notice that Jesus actually uses three slightly different words that are altogether translated as "eunuch" in the English language. Here is a short refresher of these translations.

When referring to the born-eunuch, Jesus uses the word "eunouchos," but when referring to the castrated eunuch, He uses the word "eunouxízō." Then, when referring to the one who decides to be a eunuch for the Kingdom's sake, He uses the word "eunoúxos."

While the best word in English for all three categories is the word "eunuch," there are positive reasons for why Jesus chose separate variations in His teaching.

Eunouchos – literally, "alone in bed" (i.e. without a marriage partner).

Of the three word variations Jesus used in His explanation for biblically remaining unmarried, eunouchos is the only one that is not exclusively masculine in physicality. This word is used inclusive of both men and women to designate those who are born that way. A more modern term that appears to fit nicely within the context of eunouchos, is the term "eunuchoid." This word is described as "partially resembling, or having the general characteristics of, a eunuch." So, a female can be a natural "eunuch," born with no opposite sex attraction. In some cases (though certainly not all), she may not even desire motherhood. In fact, in some regions of the middle-east, a woman who is sterile, or even postmenopausal, may still become labeled as a "eunuch."

Expectations

Little girls raised in Christian homes are often taught early in life to wait for "Mr. Right." They are told, "Just have patience and God will send him along. Someday, your knight in shining armor will come and sweep you off your feet." That "someday" comes and goes, and while most of her friends have married and started families, she now feels like a second-class citizen among all the blushing brides.

While we should teach our daughters the principles of courtship, we should also be teaching them the principles of being "honorably unmarried." Even if a child will one day marry, each will have a time in life where they should be faithful in their unmarried state; this is beneficial for everyone. Contentment versus frustration is a tug-of-war between how you feel and how everyone says you should feel. "What kind of woman does not want to be a wife and mother?" you might ask. Many times even parents succumb to this confusion (I certainly have). We teach our daughters to be content in whatever state the Lord puts them, but then we spend years conditioning them and equipping them only to be capable wives and mothers, as if there is no other possible alternative.

Is there a biblical role for unmarried women in the church and in society? Absolutely. Just as there is a special role for the unmarried male, there is a special role for unmarried women within our churches. Let me share some thoughts regarding these female eunuchs.

Faithfully Unmarried

The Apostle Paul states, *"There is a difference also between a wife and a virgin. The unmarried woman careth for the things of the Lord, that she may be holy both in body and in spirit: but she that is married careth for the things of the world, how she may please her husband"* (1 Corinthians 7:34).

This is not to say that married people cannot focus on God's work, but their focus is going to be different because of the necessary spousal, parental, and extended family duties they have. The unmarried woman is "free" in this sense to concentrate on God's work, helping families and giving of her time more liberally than the married woman often can.

Ministry of the Female Eunuch

We often think that ministry is only a "real" ministry if we are preaching, teaching, flying to foreign lands and leading multitudes of people to Christ. However, we should reconsider that notion if we are going to be scripturally correct. For example:

- Lydia was a gracious host and invited the church to meet in her home (Acts 16:14, 15).
- Dorcas sewed garments for the poor (Acts 9:36-40).

Our culture is demeaning to holiness and femininity. If it is not "glamorous," we ignore it as "mundane" or beneath us. This thinking is a far cry from anything Jesus ever taught. Our Lord said, "Whosoever will be great among you, let him be your minister; And whosoever will be chief among you, let him be your servant" (Matthew 20:26b, 27).

Some of the finest missionaries in the world have been unmarried women, such as Gladys Aylward, Mary Slessor, and Amy Carmichael. Some of the greatest workers in churches and Christian ministries have been unmarried women. It is not unusual to hear more about men because they usually are the face of a ministry. However, if you name any great ministry or any greatly used man, you will often discover a woman or two who played huge roles in the success of that ministry.

The Proverbs 31 "Women"

Proverbs 31 is considered the greatest description of female godliness in Scripture. Not only is she a wife, she is a super-woman. Further examination of this woman would be intimidating to any woman. For example:

- She completely satisfies her husband.
- She gets all the laundry washed and put away.
- She does all the grocery shopping.
- She is up before the kids.
- She gardens.
- She runs a successful business.
- She exercises daily.
- She stays up late and works.
- She operates a mission for the poor.
- She is not afraid of the dark.
- She is always dressed for success.
- She is a fashion designer.
- Her husband is famous *because of her*.
- She is well educated.
- And she never takes a break.

How could a wife measure up to this? The common view here is that there is one woman in this passage who is a wife. In verse 15, however, notice that it says the Proverbs 31 woman has "maidens." Maidens? Yes— faithfully unmarried ladies. Many are female eunuchs. How many thousands of "maidens" are at a loss in ministry because no one has known
100

them for whom they are and because no one has shown them what they are capable of doing?

Female Stereotypes

Our modern society often wants to stereotype women by either casting them as sex objects or making them seem masculine. I have even met young women who feel like they are not normal because they have no desire to be sensual. While a young lady may never experience the same type of societal pressure as a man for being unmarried, she will be stereotyped nonetheless. In some cultures, it may be worse. She may be seen as a spinster or a "lesbian" simply for remaining unmarried. However, our focus should never be the world's focus.

While the vast majority of young girls marry and have families of their own, there are some who will not. There are those who are called to remain unmarried for life (1 Corinthians 7:7-10). If you are a female and you identify with Matthew 19:11-12, your identity should be as a servant of Christ, who happens to be a woman.

Made to Rule, With Man

The Bible is clear that woman was made to rule with man. Genesis 1:26 says, "let *them* have dominion..." When God called the Woman a "help" to Adam, the Hebrew word used of her is the same word used elsewhere in scripture to describe the help of military reinforcement and the help of God Himself. Woman is truly a mighty design of God, not to be taken lightly.

According to Genesis 1:26, every woman's purpose is to rule with man in order to bring glory to God. Throughout the Bible, it seems, one of her responsibilities is to help the men in her life, whether he be a husband, a father, an elder, a pastor, or a protective brother. Nevertheless, it is not a degrading role. Again, the woman's help is comparable to military might and to the help of God Himself. It is in her power to care for things to see them blossom. Whatever she is given, God has enabled a woman to multiply and increase.

That is easy to understand for one who becomes a wife, but it is equally true of the female eunuchs. While they possess no sexual attraction to men, they are still empowered to bringing about success through their labors. That is why so many female eunuchs are a blessing to ministries. Female eunuchs possess much the same maternal instincts that other women possess, and many of these ladies have effective ministries with children, or other women, or the elderly. Having no sexual desire for men does not mean she lacks a desire to nurture or help others. Rather, her focus is to be turned toward God.

What Women Want

The female eunuch has been called into service to Christ. Her nurturing instincts and ability to empathize with people will be turned towards strengthening the Kingdom of God in the kingdom of men. She is, in effect, a sister and mother to many people instead of to only one family. Her capacity to teach and to relate to other people is immense. What she wants is to have many strong relationships that she can nurture.

She doesn't necessarily desire to be a wife to a husband, but she can willingly submit to God and godly authority, just as every believer is commanded to do unto each other (Ephesians 5:21). She may or may not feel the need to have children, but she has no problem investing in the futures and lives of other people as she would her own children. What does the female eunuch want? She wants strong, deep, and meaningful relationships with people. She wants the freedom to invest in those relationships. *This is a legitimate calling and should not be dismissed.*

Some who have identified themselves as "lesbian" may find that they were not born to remain unmarried. Some do in fact want to marry and bear children of their own. This confusion, as mentioned already, has arisen from a twisted view of what is attractive to men. We call these women "cultural lesbians."

Generally, we have found that fewer female eunuchs are pressured to enter the unnatural lifestyle. For some women in the "lesbian" community, though not for all, their purpose for being there (sometimes even

102

subconsciously) is because they distrust or have grown tired of men who have hurt them. In the course of trying to reach "lesbian" communities, the pastor or ministry leader will encounter this type of woman. To help these women, it is important to understand their desires and the motives that drive their actions.

Dealing With the Cultural "Lesbian"

It is important to understand a woman's sexuality and attraction. *In general, a woman is not usually attracted to a man in the same way a man is attracted to a woman.* A man looks at a woman and sees beauty. He sees something he yearns for, something he wishes to touch and gaze upon (unless he is a eunuch). A woman looks on a man and sees something entirely different. She sees someone who may take care of her, someone who can provide security, and someone who can desire her. She may be more interested in a man's personality than his physique.

- *To this end, a woman is not always looking for a man she is attracted to, but she is looking to attract a man to herself.*
- *She wants to attract a man who desires her. She wants to be desired. She wants to be the desire of his eyes (Ezekiel 24:16).*
- *But when her perception of this is skewed, then her mannerisms and attempts to attract a man are likewise skewed and perverse.*

For the women who desire men, there are *four* distinct areas of *masculinity* that *influence* her attempts to attract a man. *If any of these areas are skewed, likewise her efforts to be attractive will be skewed.*

1. ***Man's Desire: What turns him on?*** Think about this: why does a woman dress provocatively? She wants to be beautiful and this provocative manner of dressing is how our culture has taught her she must dress in order to be attractive in the eyes of men. Whatever she perceives is attractive, she will do, because she wants to be desired. This is not just true of the world. It is true in our churches as well. We need to first teach our men what they should desire (the biblical woman) and then teach our women to

103

attract a man with the right desires. When a man desires the wrong things and abuses a woman, the abused may choose to make herself less attractive as a means of protecting herself.

2. ***Man's Direction: What does he do?*** What's his purpose? Again, we must start with the men and teach them to have a godly purpose and direction in life. Godly women will find themselves wanting to attract a godly man. She will adapt the manner in which she attempts to attract him in such a way that is pleasing to God. But an ungodly woman will resort to ungodly methods to attract an ungodly man. Regardless, it still starts with the men. If the men live ungodly lives, then our women resort to ungodly methods to attract them.

3. ***Man's Duty: Why does he do what he does?*** This reasoning is important to a woman. She wants to know him. She wants to know what makes a man tick. She wants to know if she can count on him to perform his duty to her. She is looking for a man who is trustworthy and reliable, but if this area is perverted in men, she will resort to skewed methods in order to force him to be what he is not. This creates all sorts of problems in marriages, but also in a woman's attempts to attract a man.

4. ***Man's Dominance: Will he be able to protect me?*** Will she feel secure with him? It does not mean she is unable to take care of herself, but a woman attempts to attract a man that will make her feel secure. A weak masculine culture will produce strange mannerisms in the women trying to attract a man.

As you may have determined, female sexuality and attraction react in response to the right masculine culture. We must first start raising the standard with the men so that our women are attracting the single man in a godly manner.

Nevertheless, a woman may lack a desire for men altogether. Some may have been hurt or abused, others may have grown to distrust, and some may have been born to remain faithfully unmarried. No matter where they find themselves, none of them are useless or worthless. God has a purpose for their life and offers true fulfillment to those in service to Him.

Accepting the Call

One thing is certain: We need to be teaching our young girls what God expects from us all. Some are created for marriage and some are not, yet we have all been created to honor the Lord.

History is filled with examples of female eunuchs. No work of God can function as well without them. If God has called you to such a ministry, or if you were born that way, do not feel like you are incomplete or less of a woman than any other.

Chapter Twelve
LONELY EUNUCHS

Is it loneliness that led Sam into the trap of the "gay" lifestyle? If so, wouldn't it seem that his loneliness would drive him back to the same lifestyle again. Loneliness is not what causes most eunuchs to fall away into sin, but the feeling of not being accepted does. Acceptance is what we all crave. Loneliness is a very misunderstood concept and, if one is not careful, they can talk themselves into the illusion of a loneliness that really is not there.

- Loneliness is being misunderstood in the world where you live.
- Loneliness is not being accepted by those around you.
- Loneliness is being rejected and left to deal with your hurt alone.
- Loneliness is not having another with whom to share life's experiences.

A widow may miss her husband and not be lonely as long as there is a place where she is loved and accepted and where there are people with whom she can find fellowship. It is not her aloneness that creates loneliness, but the feeling that she does not fit in somewhere.

We often attribute other feelings to loneliness. For example:

- Sorrow is not loneliness.
- Homesickness is not loneliness.
- Separation is not loneliness.
- Grief over a lost loved one is not loneliness.
- Depression is not loneliness.

All these feelings may accompany loneliness, but we must not mistake them for loneliness. The life of a eunuch is not a sentence for loneliness, and in fact, can be quite the contrary. A eunuch can live a rich life void of significant loneliness, even without other eunuchs in his or her life. There are many who discover the truth that they are eunuchs who are the only one in their world.

We have all experienced some degree of loneliness, yet often it was not being alone that made us lonely, but it was not being accepted by those around us. We may be the most unique person in a crowd, and not be lonely because others have accepted us in our uniqueness. Loneliness has nothing to do with solitude. You can be *alone* without being lonely. Being alone is different than *feeling* alone. Remember these things:

1. God is not the author of loneliness, although there are times when He allows aloneness to come into our lives. Aloneness is when we are in solitude away from the crowd or from those we love. God is our substance in those times. He promises that He will never leave us nor forsake us. He is always there and His Spirit indwells us to give us peace, and where there is peace, there is no loneliness.

2. Do not seek sexual fulfillment as a cure for loneliness. Many sexually active individuals are lonely. In fact, sex has nothing to do with curing loneliness. Do not assume that intimacy is the solution. Loneliness is always found in sin's lifestyle. The end of sin is always death, also known as separation.

3. Do not mistake marriage as a cure for loneliness. There are many married individuals who suffer loneliness because they do not feel accepted in their home. Do not feel you must be married in order to not be lonely. I discuss more on the subject of marriage in another chapter that helps to clear up the confusion on the subject of "gay marriage."

4. Building meaningful relationships is a cure for loneliness. All humans are created to be in relationships. We are designed to connect with other people. Every significant event in our life is on some level emotional and relational—birth, friendship, employment, salvation, church, and even death to name a few.

5. Loneliness is a warning that we are not properly connected to God. Loneliness is like a hunger pang; it is an emotional warning that something is missing. It is a spiritual disconnection. A person who experiences perpetual loneliness has often suffered a great loss of some kind. The thought of being hurt again causes them to withdraw, even from the Lord; therefore, their cure becomes a threat. The answer is in reaching out to the Lord as we see in His Word.

Psalm 68:4-6 – *Sing unto God, sing praises to his name: extol him that rideth upon the heavens by his name Jah, and rejoice before him. A father of the fatherless, and a judge of the widows, is God in his holy habitation. God setteth the solitary in families: he bringeth out those which are bound with chains: but the rebellious dwell in a dry land.*

God responds to His own when we sing unto Him, when we praise Him, when we extol or magnify Him, and when we rejoice in His presence. It is then that God comes and heals the loneliness within us.

6. God's grace is sufficient to prevent aloneness from becoming loneliness. The Apostle Paul, a self-proclaimed eunuch, suffered many things, and no doubt there were probably times when Paul fought loneliness. We know he was often alone or rejected by those around him. Yet, Paul maintained a less than lonely demeanor as we see in this oft quoted passage.

Romans 8:35 – *Who shall separate us from the love of Christ? Shall tribulation, or distress, or persecution, or famine, or nakedness, or peril, or sword?*

Many people suffer loneliness as a result of their feelings of separation. Paul shared the many ways he suffered, but he held onto the truth that nothing separates us from God's love. Eunuchs who fear loneliness need not fear because they are not alone. God in His sufficiency can sustain them in their aloneness and prevent them from living the life of a lonely eunuch.

Perhaps the greatest cause of loneliness is isolation. When a man or woman concludes that they were born as a eunuch, they must make the conscious choice not to isolate themselves from others. You are not strange; you are unique, but aren't we all? God made each of us to be

109

conformed into His image, but in a unique way. Each of us must accept our uniqueness with gratitude to the Lord and not isolate ourselves into a world of self-pity.

You have not been relegated to a lonely life, my eunuch friend. The life God has chosen for you can be filled with rich relationships as you give your life to others in service to our Lord.

Chapter Thirteen
THE LIFE OF A EUNUCH

We all have preconceived ideas about what constitutes a fulfilled life versus a wasted life. For those who see things from an earthly perspective, it would be easy to see how they might think that a life like Sam's would be a wasted life. In fact, this is one of the most difficult things families of eunuchs often face. They think that their eunuch son or daughter never knowing the joys of marriage or parenthood is a tragedy. They see marriage and parenthood as that which gives meaning to life.

An Alabaster Box

A prominent preacher, who is also a eunuch, was issuing a challenge to those in the audience who were unmarried. His message had been on the story of the woman with the expensive alabaster box of ointment. She broke the alabaster box open and poured the ointment on the head of Jesus. She was summarily reprimanded by some who were there. In fact, they were indignant about the action she had taken because they felt the money could have been sold to feed the poor. In essence, what they said about her sacrifice was, "What a waste."

In Matthew 19, Christ warned His disciples that there would be many who would think it a waste to live their lives as a eunuch. The Apostle Paul told of personally being reviled by those who thought that he was wasting his life being unmarried, but he knew that it was the sacrifice he had made for the sake of Christ. He encouraged others to do the same thing.

Life of a Eunuch

Many people cannot grasp the beauty of a eunuch's life, yet those who have lived such a life find it to be rich and full. Was the life of the Apostle John a waste? Did the Apostle Paul waste his life by remaining unmarried?

History is filled with the stories of those who chose to "waste" their lives in this lifestyle. There are several attributes that define such a life.

It is a life of commitment. Being a eunuch is not for the flippant and shallow. This life, though rich in blessings, does require sacrifices that others do not have to make. They will at times be alone and even experience loneliness. They will not know what it is like to be called mommy or daddy by a child of their own, although they are often greatly compensated by the vast number of people who look to them as a father or mother figure.

It is a life of consecration. An individual that is consecrated has been set apart for a particular purpose. A eunuch's life is a consecrated life because he has decided to replace the life of having a spouse and family with remaining unmarried to serve the Lord.

It is a life of chastity. Chastity is moral purity. One who is chaste has committed himself to remain pure. Some may argue that they have lost their chastity, but I have news for you. *Chastity is a virtue that can be lost and then regained.* One who has engaged in moral impurity can subsequently confess their sins to God and be cleansed. They can then live a life of moral purity from that point forward.

It is a life of celibacy. In the matter of celibacy, chastity is assumed. A person can be morally pure and still be married and sexually active within marriage, but celibacy is a life given over to remaining sacredly unmarried. It is when a man or woman makes a commitment to remain unmarried for the remainder of their lives. Is it possible for a person to be celibate if they have been married in the past? The answer is yes. There are some who believe that Paul had previously been married, but Paul lived out his life in celibacy.

It is a life of celebration. The eunuch's life should be celebrated by both the eunuch as well as other Christians. The eunuch celebrates his calling openly, in humility, in order to encourage others who have been called to this life. We who are not eunuchs should celebrate the special place

112

eunuchs play in our church in order to affirm their acceptance in the church as a vital part of the work of God in that local assembly.

It is a life of compassion. There is a common thread I have seen in the eunuchs with whom I have dealt. They are extremely sensitive and compassionate people. They are caregivers and servants. They love to nurture others and reach out to the underprivileged and the unloved.

It is a life of commensuration. Someone once said that life gives you what you are willing to give. In that regard, God certainly pays His servants extremely well. We cannot objectively judge the life of a eunuch that has given up what we consider to be significant pleasures of life. Their life is one of great reward. When a person has lived a life dedicated to the Lord as a eunuch, their lives will be rich and fulfilling. They will confidently look forward to that day when Jesus says, "Well done my good and faithful servant."

Do not pity the eunuch, for their life is filled with blessings and richness which others will never know. They trade the benefits of marriage and parenthood for benefits that far outweigh the sacrifices they must make. It is not a life they chose, but one they were honorably selected to live.

Chapter Fourteen
FALLACY OF
SAME SEX MARRIAGES

Options

Get married – Don't get married – Marriage is honorable – Marriage is forbidden. Imagine the confusion that is often generated in young people like Sam when they hear such statements. It would almost appear that we are a bit schizophrenic in the way we respond to this vital subject. Churches have, through the centuries, been the champion of sacred marriages. Preachers have proclaimed the truths about marriage being a God sanctioned union between a man and a woman. However, I fear that in championing it, we have also cheapened it as well. Marriage has lost its place, even in our churches. This is one of the reasons we have an element today who condone same-sex marriage.

Hebrews 13:4 – *Marriage is honourable in all, and the bed undefiled: but whoremongers and adulterers God will judge.*

Scriptural marriage is a wonderful thing. I highly recommend it to those who choose it as a lifetime commitment; however, the Bible never said that marriage is honorable for all. It says that marriage is honorable *in* all. The meaning in this passage is that marriage is to be an honored institution within the church. God honors marriage as a sacred institution where the bed (or sexual relationship) between a husband and wife is pure and without defilement. Sex outside of marriage is treated harshly and strictly forbidden by God, and He promises to judge those who partake in it.

Marriage is a choice that is honored by God. However, this does not mean marriage is honorable *for* all. This is the first mistake that many of us have made within our churches. We have treated marriage as though it were necessary for one to be in favor within the church and even with God. We

115

have taught our young people that marriage is the end of God's will, when it is not in the least true for all of them. This leaves those who remain unmarried to feel forever inferior. Terms like "old maids" are not merely insulting; they are an indication that we treat marriage as the "end all" for everyone.

The military was a good experience for me. No doubt it helped develop me into the man I am today. I recommend it to anyone who has an inclination to enlist. However, I do not recommend it to every young person who comes to me. I first get to know them in order to find out what might be best for them. I ask questions to find out if their reasons are good ones. I have known young people who were merely trying to get away from home, or something, or someone by joining the military. As a result, the military was a disaster for them. My counsel is based upon my concern for them, not my love for the military.

The same thing is true about marriage. Marriage has been a good experience for me, and I knew early on that I wanted to have a wife and family. However, what has been good for me does not mean it is going to be good for everyone. Rather than counseling every young person to pursue marriage, I treat it as an *option,* not an *automatic.*

The Seeker

Some people have stated that God favors marriage. They use Proverbs 18:22 as the basis of their argument. Solomon told his son, *"Whoso findeth a wife findeth a good thing, and obtaineth favour of the Lord."* The word "findeth," should make it clear that Solomon was suggesting that a search was taking place. When a man seeks a wife and finds her, it is a good thing. I agree completely that, if a man believes it is the right thing for him to be married, it is a good thing when his search culminates with success. However, this also indicates the seriousness of the matter of seeking a wife. This passage indicates that finding a wife was not the result of an accidental encounter, but of a diligent and thoughtful search. Not every young man should enter into that search, and if they do, it should be after serious deliberation and prayer.

The second half of this passage is often misunderstood. The Bible says that he obtained favor of the Lord, which indicates that the favor is in the finding, *not* in the fact. Let me explain. I sought for a wife because it was God's will for me to be married. When I met my wife, I was favored of God, because I had sought her with wisdom and principle. God favored me by allowing me to find her, and we have been blessed. This does not mean that a married man has more favor than an unmarried one. The man who seeks a wife and finds one does so because of the favor of God.

Nowhere in the Bible do we see a woman seeking a husband. We see men seeking a wife, but never a wife seeking a husband. When I send my daughters off to college, it will not be to find a husband, but to learn how to be good women. I do not want them trying to attract a man. If my daughters are to be married, I want it to be because a man found them while seeking for the right wife. By the way, Christ, the Bridegroom, sought us, the bride, and not vice versa. If we exemplify Him, we should see the sacredness and the seriousness with which He sought us. Jesus came to seek and to save us. Marriage should not be treated any less sacred.

The seeking woman often becomes a seductress, even in our churches. Over and over again, we see instances of men seeking a wife in the Bible, but never a woman seeking a husband. If you study all the warnings Solomon gave to his son regarding women, you will see, when independently viewed, things that are not always bad, but they do indicate a woman was the pursuer. Yet we teach our girls in church, Christian schools, and homes how to "win" a man. Then we wonder why our divorce rate mirrors that of the heathen world. Perhaps we are promoting a "Christian" version of unholy dating.

Marriage Is Not for Everyone

Let me make it clear; telling our kids that their purpose in life is to find a spouse is like me telling every young adult that they should enlist in the military. If a young man believes it is best for him to marry, then he should begin his search. That search should be principled and based upon

Scripture. He should avoid women who are aggressive flirts. He should go about it in a way that will allow God to show him favor, by leading him to a good woman. I am in no way trying to discourage marriage. Marriage is going to happen in the majority of our young people's lives, but it should be a byproduct of seeking God's purpose rather than falsely assuming it is His purpose for everyone.

Once again, we have pushed our young people into making bad choices by our misunderstanding of the truths about marriage. We have young people declaring they are "gay" because we have not addressed the issue properly. We have other marriages ending up in divorce court because of our emphasis on teaching that marriage is for everyone.

Finally, there are those who will suggest that every man and every woman is to be married if they are to be in the perfect will of God. They claim 1 Corinthians 7:2 as an edict for marriage: *"Let every man have his own wife, and let every woman have her own husband."* However, if this verse is an edict, then it would seem it is an edict for men *not* to marry because in the preceding passage. Looking at the beginning of the chapter, it begins with, *"It is good for a man not to touch a woman."* Paul was suggesting that the best thing for every man is not to get involved. However, he was echoing what Jesus said in Matthew 19 when he says, *"Nevertheless..."* Here, Paul gives the solution for those who cannot remain a eunuch as he did. Everyone who cannot live chastely unmarried or who has the desire get married should find a spouse to meet their needs.

It is interesting that, in the day Paul wrote this letter to the church at Corinth, there were many who were discouraging marriage. In fact, there were some who considered it to be a bad thing and were promoting a complete unmarried ideology for everyone to the church. They wrote to the Apostle Paul, questioning him regarding this issue, and he wrote back, starting his message with the words, *"Now concerning the things whereof ye wrote unto me."* Apparently, they had some questions and this was the one he first addressed. Had Paul suggested that every Christian should get married, he would have gone out and found a wife for himself.

118

Let me surmise briefly on what was happening here. We know that the church in Corinth was a sensual and worldly church. We also know there were moral problems within the church. Some were criticizing marriage with a pharisaical attitude. There are always those who choose a path and then try to make everyone do what they did. Most likely, the people were struggling with this issue, and Paul addressed the need for them to avoid committing fornication in order to have their sexual desires satisfied by being married. Paul was not contradicting Christ, but merely applying the same principle to a church that was struggling with the issue.

Many eunuchs are adversely affected by our common and erroneous teaching within the church because they are pushed towards the idea that they must get married. Otherwise, they are considered "lesser" people. They feel no desire towards the opposite sex in adolescence, so they feel inferior. They pretend for a while, but often end up rebelling against the position the church has taken on this subject. Although their rebellion is wrong, the position of the church led them to that attitude. We pushed marriage down their throats as though it were the best and *only* option.

The second half of Hebrews 13:4, *"Whoremongers and adulterers God will judge,"* echoes what Paul says in 1 Corinthians 7:2-3, *"Nevertheless, to avoid fornication, let every man have his own wife, and let every woman have her own husband."* Verse 3 also explains the husband and the wife have a responsibility to care for each other sexually: *"Let the husband render unto the wife due benevolence: and likewise also the wife unto the husband."* Benevolence here indicates meeting the needs of the other. So, when a man and a woman enter into marriage, it is with the understanding they are to fulfill the other's sexual needs.

How foolish would it be for a man or a woman to enter into an institution, which includes the command to fulfill their spouse's sexual needs, if one of the two of them had no sexual desire for the other? This is where we must be honest enough to admit that there are those who are not born with such desires.

The next mistake we make is that we inadvertently promote sexual desire. This is something we must deal with honestly. Without realizing it, we often promote the idea that every young person should have sexual desires. This unfortunately does two things. It promotes premature sexuality among those who were born with the desire, and it places pressure on those who were not born with desire to pretend they were.

There seems to be a sensual undertone in the way we teach our young people today. We teach our girls how to attract a man, when in the Scriptures, the only time we see women trying to attract a man is in a negative context. A woman who is what she should be will be noticed by God, and when a young man decides to seek for a wife, God will make a way to point her out to him.

A man who seeks a wife based upon Scriptural principles will feel favored by God when he finds her. A man who marries for sensual attraction is far more vulnerable to be seduced after he is married.

Perversion of Purpose

Why do people get married? I know it's the traditional thing to do, but why? Why did God create this beautiful relationship called marriage? Some people say marriage was created to solve Adam's loneliness, but was Adam lonely? Others say the purpose of marriage is for procreation, but if that's true, what do you say to all the couples who aren't able to have children? Is their marriage illegitimate? Is companionship or posterity the true purpose for the creation of marriage? Certainly, companionship and having children are good byproducts of marriage, but neither are said to be its purpose.

The Lord does give us an answer. Marriage is a mystery—God explains in Ephesians 5:31 and 32: *"For this cause shall a man leave his father and mother, and shall be joined unto his wife, and they two shall be one flesh. This is a great mystery: but I speak concerning Christ and the church."*

Did you get that? Marriage—its true purpose—had for generations been a mystery until this point. What a beautiful mystery it was too, but now the New Testament Scriptures reveal this great mystery. The purpose of marriage was (and is) to be a revelation or expression of Christ and His bride. How incredible! How wonderful!

120

Much like a little lamb in the Old Testament was a picture of Christ, so is the groom within marriage. This is an important observation because God takes His illustrations very serious. The people weren't allowed to sacrifice just any old lamb; it had to be spotless. Why? It was representing our spotless Lord!

Moses was barred entry into the Promise Land—not for getting angry, but for smiting the Rock of Horeb *twice*. God made it very clear that that particular Rock was an illustration of His Son. Christ was to be stricken *once* for man's sin, not twice! Moses had damaged God's illustration, and for that he suffered correction.

As a married man, I must understand that my marriage has a divine purpose, and that purpose is NOT my happiness or heritage. The purpose of my marriage and every other marriage is to express JESUS! In the beginning, marriage was a mystery, but not anymore. Now it's a mandate—a holy responsibility. Every married couple should examine themselves, sincerely asking, "Does our marriage exemplify Christ?"

Now just think how indignant Christ must feel when society so foolishly abandons God's beautiful and prophetic picture of man and wife with same-sex union. A diseased lamb for the altar, a twice stricken rock, and a man-man union are all the same: gross delusions of what God intended to be beautiful examples of His love.

Sadly, the bridge to sexuality is built on the tenants of sensuality, which is often acceptable in the church. Tragically, even our churches that *practice* worldly separation do not properly *teach* worldly separation. We still promote sensuality within modesty. We teach a modesty of apparel without a modesty of attitude. We teach modesty in apparel, but often leave out the principles of shyness and discretion. In other words, our girls are not to be chasing boys around and drawing attention to themselves.

The Bible goes much further than we do in this matter. In 1 Timothy 2:9 and 10, it says, *"In like manner also, that women adorn themselves in modest apparel, with shamefacedness and sobriety; not with broided hair, or gold, or pearls, or costly array; But (which becometh women professing godliness) with good works.*"

There are girls in our churches who feel inferior if they do not have a boyfriend, when perhaps we should make them feel superior. They do not need a boyfriend. At the appropriate time, they need to be the "favor" God bestows on a principled young man who is seeking a wife, **not** a girlfriend. The boyfriend/girlfriend mentality is leading to mass confusion among our young people, which then leads to bad marriages and drives those like Sam into confusion.

I contend that both the high rate of divorce and the rising rate of "homosexuality" are the result of a perversion of purpose within our homes and churches. Sexuality abounds because sensuality abounds. We build the bridge to it with the lack of teaching regarding finding the purpose of God before finding a person to date. We surreptitiously allude to the need for sex, without crossing the lines of what we deem as inappropriate. Any allusions to sexuality are wrong unless it is being taught within the principles of purity and chastity. Even then, we should do it carefully and with great emphasis on the matter of chastity being the first and foremost goal.

Perhaps, in all that we have taught, the thing that has harmed us the most is that the honor of remaining unmarried has been replaced with the *stigma* of remaining unmarried. A person who remains chaste and unmarried has a stronger focus on the purpose God has for their life. They should be applauded, not treated like leftover losers who could not find a spouse.

The pressure placed upon our young people to be "desired" is foolhardy. The pressure to have premature desires is lethal. Let them develop their desires slowly, and then address them appropriately at the right time and in a thoughtful manner. The problem with many kids today is that they have no one to discuss with them what they are feeling. Who can they trust to accept them, and who has the wisdom to guide them?

Devaluation of Marriage

Hopefully, all Christians are concerned about the treatment of marriage in making same sex unions legal in this country. However, long before society devalued this institution, the churches did so in the way we sold it to our kids. By worshiping marriage, we devalued it. Worshiping anything **not** meant to be worshiped is the same as devaluing it.

We took away the sacredness of marriage by pushing the idea that it is some kind of sensual, romantic byproduct that is somehow necessary for everyone. Would you like to see the results? Look around your church.

- Unmarried moms and dads
- Grandparents raising grandchildren
- Increase of divorce in the church
- Married kids moving back in with parents
- Immorality among married people
- Adultery

The church is filled with its own byproducts. Among the saddest of these are the confused people like Sam who end up leaving the church altogether because they have no answers as to why they do not desire a traditional family. Should it surprise us that those who leave us want the same thing we have promoted for so long...marriage? We must teach our young people that, as wonderful as marriage is, it is not to be worshiped as the pinnacle of our being.

Yes, marriage is honorable in all, but not for all. Some are born to remain faithfully unmarried.

Chapter Fifteen
ALREADY MARRIED

Many young people, like Sam, take a far more drastic step in trying to deal with their lack of attraction to the opposite sex. They follow the standard line of "every man ought to find a wife and every woman ought to find a husband." They get married in an almost desperate attempt to be accepted, as well as to hopefully "solve" their problem. Since my first meeting with Sam, I have met with many eunuchs who are already married. When they discover their true identity, it has led to some serious confusion. What should they do? Do they remain married, or do they somehow dissolve the marriage?

Let me begin by dealing with the terrible pressure that young people are under to get married. In our society, particularly in churches, we push people towards marriage, and we encourage "normal" sexual desire towards the opposite sex. Although our society has changed some, and less and less people are getting married as early, we still push our unmarried individuals into marriage. How many of them have been "set up" on a date? How many "matchmakers" exist in our churches? How many sermons are geared towards encouraging marriage and discouraging remaining unmarried? It is far more than most people realize. In fact, those who are not seeking a spouse are often stigmatized or even scandalized as being "gay" or "lesbian."

That type of environment often "pressures" someone into a marriage even when they do not have the sexual desires or attraction for their marriage partner. Some of the reasons for getting married may be to avoid the stigma of not being attracted to the opposite sex, to please parents, to stop being teased, or to be able to serve in a greater capacity within the church. As a result, married eunuchs do exist, and many of them sit in the pews of our churches suffering difficulties that few of us comprehend or even know how to address. There are a variety of reasons those with no attraction decide to get married.

1. They grew up with the reinforced message that it is not okay to remain unmarried. They have been encouraged all their life to "like" the opposite gender. Friends begin setting them up on dates and pushing them towards the marriage goal. They finally get married because they believe it is what God expects—or at least what those whom they love expect. They do not want to displease those people, so they choose to marry.

2. They love the "idea" of being married. Perhaps to them it is a mark of prestige or status that opens certain doors and opportunities denied them as an unmarried person. It is more about the idea of being married than the ideal of the individual they married.

3. It is a so-called test of "manhood" or "womanhood." Getting married proves their masculinity or femininity. They perceive marriage as a way to prove that they are "normal." People fear being different or being perceived as odd. Getting married for some is about self-confidence, security, and self-assurance.

4. Some think that marriage will "cure" their confusion or that by "trusting God" they can cope with a marriage. As Christians, they probably believed that "following the right godly path" meant getting married. They wanted to do what they thought was right, as well as be accepted in their church.

5. They have a deep, intimate connection with someone of the opposite gender (although not sexual in nature). This is not unusual. Many marry someone because they do not want to lose that friendship, rather than because they are attracted to them. Natural born eunuchs are by nature very nurturing individuals and often form deep connections that have nothing to do with sex. Sometimes, they marry just to preserve that connection.

Whatever their reasons for getting married, it is a reality that many eunuchs do. When natural eunuchs finally disclose their lack of sexual interest, there are typically two results. The first is that they declare

126

themselves "gay" or "lesbian," which often leads to divorce and plunges them into a sinful lifestyle. The second result is that it creates discord in the marriage because their spouse suddenly feels rejected, embarrassed, and fearful. This brings problems to the marriage that few pastors or counselors are equipped to cope with.

One of the main causes of divorce is intimacy issues, but how do you force someone to become sexually attracted to someone else? We often advise them to turn it over to God, expecting Him to change their desires. When that does not occur, we blame it on their lack of spirituality or on their sinful nature. We are convinced that if someone is right with God, they will develop "normal" sexual attractions towards their spouse. This does not solve their "problems," and only sets them up for failure within the marriage.

Here are some typical problems that a eunuch husband may face within the marriage:

- Fear of hurting his spouse.
- Fear of losing his spouse's love.
- Fear of being rejected by everyone else.
- Fear that something is inherently wrong with him, rendering him useless.
- Fear of being "gay." He does not have strong sexual desires towards his wife, but he probably has strong male friends, so he begins to doubt himself.
- Immersion in sinful behavior just to see if he does have the right or wrong desires. He could look at pornography or participate in other sexually deviant behaviors in an effort to truly discover himself. If pornography does not affect him, he may wonder if he is "gay" after all.
- Doubts his marriage, his love for his wife, and his purpose for living.
- Doubts God's love for someone who is "not" normal.
- Considers divorce as possibly the easiest solution to the problem.

127

- Problems with parents, friends, and children who don't understand him.

While it is true that life can be extremely tough for the eunuch who is also married, it is often the spouse of the eunuch who suffers the most. His wife goes through a different suffering dynamic. The wife jumps into the marriage with all the "normal" feelings and attractions. She wants sex and enjoys it, but now must face a situation where it will be denied her more frequently. Here are some typical problems that the wife of a eunuch may face:

- Feels that she did something wrong, that she is not a good wife.
- Feels rejected, unloved...and unlovely.
- Suffers from low self-esteem, shame, loss, and long bouts of depression.
- Can't understand her husband's lack of feelings and becomes very angry.
- Worries about getting a divorce.
- Wants a divorce because she feels betrayed and cheated.
- May become insecure and bear imaginary blame.
- Does not know how to relate to her husband anymore as she is consumed by this revelation.
- Does not understand the difference between sex and intimacy.
- May struggle with unfulfilled sexual desires.
- Feels lonely, not sure who to turn to or who to share with.

So what is the solution for these marriages? Well, let me begin by saying that divorce is not an option. That needs to be made very clear. Once a man or woman chooses to get married—regardless of their reasons—getting a divorce is wrong on many different levels. The marriage is not doomed, and there can be incredible joy in the marriage. It begins by recognizing that a marriage is not predicated on sex. A married eunuch can still be the right kind of husband to his wife even if sexuality is not present.

1. He can love and support his wife. By reassuring her that she is special to him, he can make her feel secure even as she struggles to understand the situation. Just because his "sex drive" may be lacking does not mean that he is lacking in other areas that are important to a marriage. Real, biblical love is more valid and more important than erotic love.

2. He can meet her basic needs. Everyone has some basic needs, and as a husband, a man can give his wife these three things:

To be needed. Everyone needs to be needed. Regardless if the husband is a natural born eunuch or not, if he is married, he still needs his wife. He can express that need.

To be wanted. This is not the same as needing someone. I can want something I don't need, and I can need something I don't want. Not only does a wife need to be needed, she also needs to be wanted. There are many ways a man can want his wife that does not involve sex. In fact, if that is the only way a man wants his wife, she will quickly grow discontent. A eunuch may not want his wife sexually, but there are many other ways that he can want her as part of his life. He should find ways to express this to his wife.

To be appreciated. It is possible not to appreciate something you want or need. In any marriage, it is possible to take our spouse for granted and fail to show appreciation. A married eunuch needs to show appreciation for his wife. She needs this appreciation, and a husband can provide this in many different ways.

3. He can understand the purpose for marriage. In Ephesians 5, Paul gives instructions to husbands and wives, declaring that the marriage relationship is a picture of the union of Christ with the church. The objective of marriage is to reflect the love relationship between God and His people and to implant and perfect that love in human personalities. Marriage is God's workshop, or garden, in which He is growing and maturing personalities for eternity. This objective should be recognized by every Christian couple so that the ups and downs of their marriage experience can be taken in proper stride.

God's plan is a perfect plan. In marriage, God intended for children to be born and nurtured in a home where there is love and peace. God created marriage for husbands and wives to grow in their marriage relationship and grow as human beings. God made marriage so that men and women could enjoy the sexual passions that He has given to them in a context of intimacy, love, affirmation, and commitment. God made marriage to help us understand more fully His love for us, His spiritual bride.

4. He can realize that marriage is much more than sexual activity. To be sure, a physical relationship is important in marriage, but it was not intended to be the main priority. Holy matrimony is a spiritual, emotional, mental, and physical union—not solely based on sex. If a eunuch is married, he has a partner. Involving her in his life is what a partner does. When God created Eve, He said, "It is not good that the man should be alone; I will make him an help meet for him." It does not say that God created a sex-mate. He created a help meet. If a married eunuch can see his wife in that light, he will have a much easier time accepting himself, his marriage, and his role in the marriage.

5. He can understand real love. Love is not an emotion—though it can certainly affect emotions and feelings. It is more of an action. There is great contentment when real biblical love is employed in a marriage. Seeing the wife as a best friend will enable him to give sacrificial love to her, to put her needs above his own. Understanding this truth will help shape his attitude and perspective towards the marriage.

Note: The problem examples and recommendations given above specify the eunuch husband with a wife; however, the roles may be reversed and equally apply to a eunuch wife with a husband.

One of the unique challenges eunuchs face is self-rejection. They have battled their feelings for years, trying to come to grips with the fact that they don't have the "normal" feelings that everyone else claims to have. Before knowing the biblical truths, they often descend into depression, self-pity, and a great deal of introspection. Internalized guilt is very common as one begins to worry about being deviant or "gay," but also about whether or not they should have gotten married to begin with. All of these feelings will leave their mark on a marriage.

When a married eunuch does not understand his or her proper role in a marriage relationship, it is easy to qualify feelings with the only thing that "might" make sense: "the gay/lesbian lifestyle." Soon their minds travel down that road as one begins to mentally rationalize these thoughts. If not stopped, this can lead to a shattered marriage and an abandoned relationship with God. In some cases, it can plunge one into the realm of sexual sin—lust, porn, adultery, homosexual behavior, and so on—all in an effort of finding that "climax" of intimacy they feel they are missing out on.

However, once a eunuch can achieve the proper perspectives, he or she will be on the way to discovering how to love their spouse in the proper manner. Both individuals will then be able to find contentment and peace in their marriage. But so much of this contentment is predicated on having the right perspective and attitude towards the marriage. Seeing it in a biblical light is the first step forward in this process.

Chapter Sixteen
REMOVING MISPLACED CONDEMNATION

The same night Sam received the truth and found his purpose, the Lord began to burden my heart for the multitudes of secret sufferers like Sam. When the chains of distortion and confusion were broken in Sam's life, he asked a question that, quite honestly, I could not answer. He asked, *"Preacher, why didn't someone show this to me when I was younger?"* Since that night, it has been my goal to find the answers to Sam's question.

Shortly after I taught the principles of eunuchs in a church, a pastor said, "I wish I had been aware of these truths twenty years ago." He proceeded to tell me the story of a young man who had been in his church many years before. He had come to the pastor pleading for help and understanding. He confessed that he felt no attraction to girls and it confused him. The pastor advised the young man to change the way he behaved. He tried to remold him into his image of a "woman-loving man." He suggested that if he found a girl to marry then everything would be fine.

That young man did exactly that. However, instead of one life being affected, now there were two. The pastor's solution did not work, and both the young man and his new wife became bitter as they realized the truth. Eventually, she left her husband and the church. The young man left the church and turned to a homosexual lifestyle. The pastor felt like he had fai ed both individuals because their lives were deeply hurt. Churches all across America have felt the sting of one who has turned away from the faith to follow after the gay lifestyle. Confusion enters the church as they deal with how to approach this situation. Likewise, many people have felt the sting of rejection from the church when they have made this choice. Often, it is not the choice they wanted to make, but the only one they believed was viable. It leaves them asking the question, "Why has my church abandoned me in my time of need?"

As a pastor, I grieve for those on both sides of the issue, the church and the one choosing to leave. I grieve for the ones who are leaving because it is not always a choice to abandon their church family. Most people, like Sam, do not want to leave their church, but they feel there is no place for them. In most cases, it is not a choice they want to make. Please do not misunderstand me; all of us wish we could choose our sins and still be in good standing with our church and with God, but that is not possible. However, this is especially true with those who leave because they have determined they are "gay."

Consequences

Leaving the church is a choice filled with consequences. Sam knew the price he would pay for his choice, and it was not a price he wanted to pay, but he felt that the consequences of living a lie would be even worse.

It is also a choice with unknown repercussions. A young person who grows up in the church has no idea what lies ahead for him when he decides to change his lifestyle.

I also grieve for the church which watches a member proclaim they are "gay" and then leaves. Few churches are prepared to deal with this type of situation. Most pastors have a heart for sinners while maintaining a hatred for sin. The conflict is often difficult. Sam's pastor loved Sam and that did not change. However, he could not look the other way and ignore the sin Sam was choosing. Many good and loving churches simply do not understand the significance that Jesus placed on those who are born eunuchs.

Try to see this scenario from two perspectives:

First, how would a young man feel growing up in this kind of church if he were born a eunuch?

Secondly, how would the members of this kind of church family feel confronting a young man whom no one understands and at the same time being ignorant concerning Matthew 19:12?

This happens all too often within Christianity. There has been a sly strategy on the part of our spiritual enemy. God says perfect love will cast out all fear (1 John 4:18). Since that is true, our enemy, Satan, has tried his best to inject mankind with fear. If perfect love casts out all fear, fear will undoubtedly cast out perfect love.

A War

Today there is a war going on between the homosexual community and churches. The war grows more severe every day. As a result of our ignorance, we are not proactive with those who may have been born as eunuchs, and they are then lost to the homosexual lifestyle. There are so many that may have been salvaged, if only our churches would have known how to deal with this problem and offer help instead of adding to the confusion. As a result, many churches did what they thought was right, and many eunuchs followed what they thought was the only option they had available.

Let me begin with the church. Twenty or thirty years ago as of the writing of this book, homosexuality existed, but it had not fully "come out of the closet." Churches were not under pressure to accept homosexuals in the church. Most people still considered homosexuality to be abnormal and sinful behavior. Preachers could call sin, "sin," without fear of repercussions. Society was not championing homosexuals as heroes for coming out. It was a different world.

Today, all of that has changed dramatically. We are in a war of beliefs that has left many preachers somewhat off guard and caused them to be *reactionary*. Calling sin by name has morphed into calling sinners names. Many preachers are caught up in the rhetoric of words that once would have been deemed as acceptable, but which is now considered as hate speech.

Preachers are being pressured to accept homosexuals into the church and are threatened if they preach that homosexuality is a sin. Political correctness has made us fearful of what we say or at least of how we say it. Those who refuse to bow are being ridiculed and threatened with actions against them.

No Answers

Unfortunately, the churches were not aware of the answer. We awoke to a society that not only embraces homosexuality, but also encourages it. Many believed Matthew 19, and some even saw its potential to address the issue, but they did not know how to apply it practically to address those who had been caught up in the gay lifestyle.

Some within the church were being drawn away into that life. This led to stronger reactions from pastors. Those who declared themselves to be gay were perceived to be a threat to others in the church. Suddenly, there was no redemption for these individuals. Pastors were in a dilemma for which they had no answer.

Another interesting phenomenon took place. People within some churches began to be sympathetic toward the newly declared gay. They knew they were different, and they felt compassion toward them, even though they did not agree with their sin. This brought confusion within church membership and, in some cases, even created strife and divisions. Much of this sympathy came from those who wondered how God could condemn the person who was **obviously** different. There was a sense that maybe *they were born different*, which we now see is true. However, what was missed by nearly all was that rather than being born "gay," they were born eunuchs. Few understood that.

A pastor is caught between two powerful forces. One is the truth of the Word of God. The other is the people who have been entrusted to his care. A good pastor spends a lifetime trying to maintain the proper balance and commitment to both. Does he shear the sheep or skin those who do not comply with the Scriptures, or does he ignore the Scripture to which they do not comply? As a pastor, I have felt the struggle of being a faithful steward of the Word and being a compassionate shepherd to the flock. The answer is simple; a pastor must go to the Bible to find the answers for the needs of the sheep.

Satan knows this, and he does his best to prevent us from finding the answers people need. Satan knew that this would be a catalyst issue in our day. He knew that few things would destroy a people like the open acceptance or even the propagation of homosexuality. Make no mistake; unnatural affection (homosexuality and lesbianism) is an *abominable sin to God*. He looks with great anger on a nation that accepts and even promotes this sin. So, what did Satan do? He stole an important truth right out from underneath us.

- Much damage has been done because of the careless behavior of some churches and pastors.
- Some claim that a person who is a "homosexual" cannot be saved until they have abandoned and forsaken their sin.
- Some declare that once a person has committed a homosexual act, they can never be forgiven because God has given them over to their sin.
- There is the name-calling of those caught in the trap of this sin such as "faggots," "queers," etc.
- Some have been treated abusively, verbally, emotionally, and in some cases physically by some in the church.
- On occasion, some have been publicly humiliated by pastors who somehow felt this would shame them back into righteousness and put fear into others in the church to deter them from following this evil path.
- Many have been voted out of the church, not with love, but with vicious hatred and unkindness.
- These "outcasts" are often shunned in public by the members.
- Yes, there have been serious wrongs committed against some of these sinners. I wish it was not the case, but sadly it is. However, there are some answers for those who have been wronged and abused.

- Christ never let you down, nor did He ever stop loving you or caring for you.
- Many Christians did not feel hatred towards you, even though they felt strongly about the wrongness of your sin.
- Most of those who mistreated you did not do so because they were trying to do evil, but because they were reacting to your sin.
- Churches are struggling to find answers just as you are trying to find answers.

Satan Buried Our Truth

It may sound strange to say the truth was buried, but let me explain. The Roman Catholic Church teaches that certain restrictions apply to those who minister God's Word. The "Priest" and the "Nun" must remain celibate. According to Catholicism, a man shepherding God's people should not have children. Their belief regarding celibacy is somewhat founded on Matthew 19:12 where Jesus describes one who chooses to become a eunuch for "the kingdom of heaven's sake." What they neglect to note however, is the fact that Jesus says, "He that is able to receive it, let him receive it." So, if someone is not "born that way," they still may choose to live a life of unmarried consecration for the ministry's sake or they may choose to get married. It's their choice.

1847 was the first big year of what is known historically as the "Irish Potato Famine." It is also the year that a Boston newspaper boldly proclaimed, "The Catholics Have Arrived." Within a few short years, nearly a million Catholics arrived in the United States. It was not long before the descendants of the English Puritans and these newly sworn citizens became aware of some vast theological differences. One of the greatest differences was "Priestly Celibacy." What happened next was spiritual civil-war. Some good things came out of this. For example, both sides redefined more about who they were and what they believed. However, the collateral damage was unfortunate.

The American Protestants fought so hard against the Catholic teaching of celibacy that they subconsciously shot and buried the doctrine regarding those who are born as eunuchs. Rather than properly explaining the scriptural principle of celibacy, they fought the idea of celibacy altogether. Thus began a sad and spiritually dark age for all those who are indeed "born that way." This is how Satan stole the idea of eunuchs from our churches today. That is why it has become almost entirely a nonexistent teaching. You will be hard pressed to find a pastor who understands it, much less who teaches it to his members.

As a result, most of those who leave a church and enter the "homosexual" lifestyle do so because they feel they are out of options and answers. That is not an excuse, but it is a reason. Until you have listened to the stories of these individuals, as I have done, you cannot know the difficulty they faced knowing they were different.

Churches did not have the answers to explain why they were the way they were. Many fought their feelings for years. *They tried to be "normal."* They tried to fit in and be like they were expected to be. They dated and pretended to be interested in the opposite sex. Like Sam, they even tried to stir embers of passions that did not exist. Sometimes, they dared to come and talk to the pastor or another Christian leader. All too often, that ended in disaster and led them to more confusion and despair. Heartbroken, they gave up on believing their church had any answers for them.

Alone and confused, they left their church and drifted off into the world where Satan had someone waiting with "the answer." There, they found the love and acceptance they had longed for, but had been unable to find. The rejection was replaced with understanding and compassion. They always knew they had no attraction for the opposite sex, but Satan tricked them into believing they must be "gay." Passions were stirred and relationships were established. Finally, they felt loved by someone for the first time in a long time. They were not seeking to go into sin. Many of those who left the church are still hurting over the choices they made and are still struggling with the guilt for doing things they knew were sinful.

Unfortunately, those who left the church were looking for answers that we did not have. This saddens me. Sam was searching, but we did not have the answer. How can we condemn them when we gave them no hope? It is said that many people steal food when they finally have lost all other options for feeding their family. Rather than letting them starve, they do what they have to do in order to find them food. That is why some of these eunuchs give up and follow their impulse. They see no other option.

People who are "born that way" are often sensitive and loving people. They believe God loves them at face value, so He would not purposely do this to someone He loves if He were not willing to forgive it or even to accept it. Yes, this is a kind of "justifying the sin," but it is what many of them think. Yet, they feel the church has let them down, which has left them bitter. Since they did not find that love in their churches, they sought it elsewhere, embracing it when they thought they had found it.

Remember, God has given us all a conscience, and there will always be a persistent feeling of guilt when we knowingly do wrong. It is only when we totally ignore that guilty feeling for too long that we are abandoned by God to our own lusts. However, as long as we are alive, there is an opportunity for repentance and restoration. *God always stands ready to forgive and restore. As Christians, we must do the same.*

We must provide a way back for these people while maintaining scriptural integrity. We can accomplish this by doing the following:

- Teach the truth about eunuchs in our churches.
- Admit where we have failed them and seek to correct it.
- Stop singling out homosexuality with vicious hatred and understand that these precious souls are in bondage and God wants to set them free.
- Be careful of hateful rhetoric and hurtful treatment.
- Identify those who were born as eunuchs so that we can guide them into God's purpose for their lives.

A war is brewing in churches across America. Families and friends have been torn apart. It is not an unimportant battle. We are fighting for truth as well as for the souls of people for whom Jesus died. Churches must maintain the *right position* as well as the *right disposition*. We must *not* concede these lives so quickly.

140

Those who have left church because of the way they were treated must accept the responsibility for their own sin and return with forgiveness and understanding. Do not ask your church to condone your sin, but seek to let them know that you have repented and turned back to chastity and celibacy.

Churches, we must seek God's forgiveness in any mistreatment of those that were "born that way." We must also forgive those who have left us and pray for a chance to teach them truth and restore them to the Lord.

No Condemnation

Those individuals who were saved and have now strayed into the "gay" lifestyle are still saved and on their way to heaven. We know that they are saved and the Holy Spirit lives within them. *There is a price for sin, but the Lord will chastise His children.* Let's pray that God will convict them and bring them back to our churches where, this time, we can give the answers we did not have before.

These are some suggestions on how to minister to those who have directly or indirectly struggled and now seek understanding and/or restoration.

- Discuss the topic of eunuchs in various settings in the church.
- Seek to remove shame and combat stereotypes and myths.
- Avoid offering simplified solutions, such as the idea that increased faith, prayer, fasting, or marriage will eliminate "sexual" same-sex attraction.
- Create a culture for all members of the congregation to feel wanted and loved.
- Help the church family learn how they can become a support network and utilize the specialness of those who identify themselves as eunuchs.
- Help the individual with the following:
- Recognize that sexual sin and failure is a mortal experience, not an eternal identity.
- Learn your spiritual strengths, talents, and abilities.

141

- Realize that unworthy actions do not diminish your spiritual worth.
- Develop healthy, nonsexual relationships with trusted individuals of the same sex.
- Identify healthy friendships you have had in the past and understand what made those "healthy."
- Look for ways to help others understand how they can be reached and supported with the truth.
- Seek to restore relationships with family and friends with those where sin and misunderstanding has caused divisions.
- Forgive others who may have hurt you, and be willing to understand that they also have shortcomings.
- Identify the most common situations that lead to temptations. Understand the feelings behind those situations, such as loneliness or rejection.
- Overcome negative dispositions and temptations, such as pride, feelings of entitlement, and/or being the "victim."
- Realize that God does not use you in spite of you, but uses you because of *Him*. God created you for His special purpose.

Most of all, we must remove condemnation from those who have returned from their sin and are now walking in chastity and purity. Romans 8:1 says, *"There is therefore now no condemnation to them which are in Christ Jesus, who walk not after the flesh, but after the Spirit."* This verse applies to them just as it does to every other sinner.

In 1738, Charles Wesley penned the words to the great hymn, *And Can It Be.* In the final stanza are words that both the eunuch and our churches should embrace with great fervor.

No condemnation now I dread;
Jesus, and all in Him, is mine;
Alive in Him, my living Head,
And clothed in righteousness divine,

Bold I approach th'eternal throne,
And claim the crown, through Christ my own.

Chapter Seventeen
MACHO, MACHO MAN

Sam was a masculine young man, but he was far from being or desiring to be a "macho man" type. When he proclaimed that he was "gay," many suggested that they were not surprised. Why would they say this? It was probably because Sam was not the "macho man" type, and that led to the idea that he was a good candidate to be gay. We should always be surprised when someone says they are gay no matter what type personality they demonstrate. It is unnatural to be gay, but it was not unnatural for Sam *not* to be macho. It was how he was uniquely created by God.

In the 1970's, during the disco craze, there was a song called Macho Man, performed by a group known as the Village People. The lyrics repeatedly say, "I've got to be a macho man." Interestingly enough, the six members of this band were purportedly all gay men and the song was more of a parody against the macho man ideal.

The word macho has become a staple of our culture for the past several decades and is derived from the word "machismo," which is defined by Wikipedia as *"a negative descriptor of, for example, sexism, misogyny, chauvinism and hypermasculinity and hegemonic masculinity. Scholars characterize such macho men as violent, rude, womanizing, and prone to alcoholism; domineering through intimidation, seducing and controlling women and children through violence and intimidation."*

While some of those descriptions may be partially present in a Christian man, much of it is the opposite of what a man is supposed to be. Unfortunately, many in the Christian world define manhood more like this than we realize. There is a "macho man" mentality that pervades many of our churches, perhaps as a reaction to the feminizing of manhood as we see it today. We teach our boys to be "macho" in the way we train them. We label those who are not manly as being "wimps" or "sissies." We stereotype manhood by the world's standard more than by God's. I have even heard some people claim that Jesus was some type of a macho man. While He was strong and even masculine, He was in no way a "macho man." He was a *complete* man, perfect in all aspects.

The result of this attitude about manhood has produced two dangerous reactions:

1. We have produced men with a careless and irresponsible attitude of macho toughness. Many of these men treat women as objects and second class citizens.

2. We have seen a trend towards the feminization of men who do not identify themselves as being macho. Some men who were masculine and strong, but not macho, have gone to the extreme of being hyper-feminine.

We are often people of extremes, and typically, extremes are dictated by our fears. We fear being "gayish," so we go to the extreme to be a macho man. Then when a young man decides he is not "straight," he begins a transformation to the extreme opposite and becomes more flamboyant in his feminine attributes. Both are reactions to our emotions. *What we fear should not define us.*

We should all be seeking to become more like Christ by the work of the Holy Spirit in our lives. However, lest we forget; we were uniquely created by God. We were not mass produced. We see in the disciples that they were similar, yet distinctly different. Therefore, while we may possess the same qualities, these qualities will manifest themselves differently based upon our uniqueness.

Real Manhood

Manhood should not be an arbitrary principle. It should not be reactionary, nor should it be based upon societal norms. Jesus was anything but normal. He was unique. He was not what everyone expected Him to be. Yet, He was the perfect man, and we are to be like Him.

Unfortunately, many people paint a portrait of Christ that is more what they *want* Him to be, rather than one that reflects what He was. Jesus was amazing. He did not merely change a man; he transformed them into what they were created to be. He said, *"Follow me and I will make you..."* (Matthew 4:19a). He took men from what they were and developed them into what they could be. In many ways, the Apostle Peter was the same man before he knew Christ as he was after, but in other ways, he was a *new* man. His personality may not have been changed, but his perspective was certainly changed. The Apostle John is a good example of a man who was a stark contrast to Peter, but he too was committed to Christ. Both of these men were unique in many ways, but similar in others.

If we look back to the way man was created, we do not see Adam as a man who came up to the serpent and asked, "What are you doing talking to my wife?" Instead, we see a man who responded to his wife without a macho type of attitude. When she gave him the fruit, he did not refuse it with the attitude, "No woman is going to tell me what to do." He took it and ate. He was not a hunter because he did not eat meat. He was not a fighter because there were no natural predators. Yet, Adam was created in the image of God. Jesus was called the second Adam. Jesus, in His manhood, was the epitome of what the first Adam was before the Fall.

When Jesus came, His life was the absolute antithesis of what people were expecting of the Messiah.

- He rebuked Peter for using his sword to cut off the servant's ear.
- He washed other men's feet.
- He allowed John to lie on his chest.
- He did not fight for his life.
- He loved little children and enjoyed their coming to Him.
- He cooked and prepared meals.
- He felt comfortable in a healing capacity with hurting people.
- He was sensitive to the touch of people.
- He noticed a lily and a sparrow.
- He could walk great distances with great stamina, but was tender with a fallen woman.

- He was a carpenter.
- He spoke with great gentleness and kindness.
- He wept openly.
- He went about doing good.
- He was not out to conquer, but to seek and to save.

Let's face it; the biblical Jesus does not match up with the modern idea of a "macho man."

Some men have taken the means to accomplish something and turned it into the end. Let me give you an example: a dad takes his son out and teaches him to hunt. That is a wonderful thing to do, but not because every boy needs to hunt. It is a mistake to make hunting the end. We brag, "My boy killed his first deer." Rather than hunting being the end, it should be a good means to an end, which is to teach our sons about Christ and help them develop the right attributes of manhood—which does not necessarily include hunting.

We often use sports to teach our boys to be victorious athletes rather than teaching them how to be virtuous men. Organized sports are not bad, but we often applaud the accomplishments of athletics to the exclusion of their purpose, which has created a generation of men who win for applause, rather than for the purpose. It has also created a stereotype of manhood that makes professional athletes an example of what we think a man should be. It has also permeated our Christian culture to the point where a fine young man like Tim Tebow is thrown to the secular wolves because he embodies so-called Christian manhood. Thank God for Christian men who happen to be great athletes, but the two are not mutually inclusive nor are they mutually exclusive. All Christians should use every opportunity to give glory to God like Tim has done in his life. However, while Tim may be a fine Christian man, the fact that he is great athlete has nothing to do with his Christianity.

The mistake is that we have used secular standards to promote manhood. We want our Christian men to show the same fruit the world does while honoring Christ. The fruit of manhood becomes success, wealth, fame, achievement, power and winning—and, oh yes, for the "glory" of the Lord too. We want our Christian men to have a trophy wife and a winning life exactly like the world. Young men are indoctrinated that the fruit of manhood is the same things as the world promotes. The fruit of godly manhood is a far cry from that which we see promoted today.

Ephesians 4:11-16 – *And he gave some, apostles; and some, prophets; and some, evangelists; and some, pastors and teachers; For the perfecting of the saints, for the work of the ministry, for the edifying of the body of Christ: Till we all come in the unity of the faith, and of the knowledge of the Son of God, unto **a perfect man**, unto the measure of the stature of the fulness of Christ: That we henceforth be no more children, tossed to and fro, and carried about with every wind of doctrine, by the sleight of men, and cunning craftiness, whereby they lie in wait to deceive; But speaking the truth in love, may grow up into him in all things, which is the head, even Christ: From whom the whole body fitly joined together and compacted by that which every joint supplieth, according to the effectual working in the measure of every part, maketh increase of the body unto the edifying of itself in love.*

The Apostle Paul, under the inspiration of the Holy Spirit, speaks of the perfect man. This description is broken down into four parts:

Part One: The Purpose of a Man

We are to do everything to the glory of God (1 Peter 4:11). A man is made to contribute to the work of God in a variety of ways, but inevitably, every Christian man is to be involved in "the work of the ministry." That is how we fulfill our purpose. Not all men are called into full time service, but every man is to be involved in some work of ministry. He may work a job to allow him to do so, but he needs to commit himself and pursue God's particular purpose for his life. Some are then called for full time Christian service and will help teach others to fulfill their purpose.

Jesus, the God/Man, exemplified this at a young age. When He was chided by his parents for not being with them, He said, *"Wist ye not that I must be about my Father's business?"* He already knew His purpose was to seek and to save that which was lost, thus He was already pursuing that purpose in His actions.

Part Two: The Character of a Man

Paul lists these three critical attributes in the character of the man:

- Maturity: *"That we henceforth be no more children..."*
- Stability: Not *"tossed to and fro, and carried about with every wind of doctrine."*
- Trustworthy: *"But speaking the truth in love..."*

Real manhood is represented by putting aside childish behavior and being stable and trustworthy, but today, men play in order to excel at playing. Playing is no longer a means to an end. It is the end in our society. Unfortunately, we allow the games they play to define their manhood, so if a young man is not good at sports, he is considered to be un-manly.

Part Three: The Fruit of Manhood

When a man knows his purpose and has the right character, he will grow in the attributes of Christ. There are those who define Jesus more by their ideas about manhood than they do by the real Jesus. We want Him to fit into our idea of manhood. We want Him to be our idea of the sinless John Wayne. Jesus was unlike any man we have ever known, yet men were attracted to Him. His manhood made everyone comfortable with Him except phonies. Jesus was not a macho man, but He was all man. He was masculine in the way that masculinity was meant to be.

In the Bible, God expresses the desire that we *"may grow up into him in all things, which is the head, even Christ"* (Ephesians 4:15). We are to grow up in Christ in all things, the things of Him. The things of Him are the fruit of His Spirit. We are not to emulate other men. We are to become like Jesus, *as we grow up in Him.* They are not the qualities of a "macho man," but the qualities of a Spirit-filled man. We see these qualities described in Galatians 5 as the fruit of the Spirit. These are the qualities that show us the Lord. After all, it is His Spirit that fills us and these qualities describe Him.

150

Quite frankly, most of these qualities are the opposite of what our society and our churches define as manhood. In fact, the qualities we see in Galatians are often those we see in people like Sam who are born eunuchs. These are not your typical macho man type of qualities.

Loving: Love is assigned to romance by Satan, not by God. In fact, love is commanded in the Bible after marriage, not before. We are not to marry because we "fall in love" or because we get a warm, fuzzy feeling about someone. That is not love. Love is obedience to God. Romantic love is the shallowest of all things described as love, because it is based on how we feel, not on what is right. A man in Christ and growing up in Him will love because he is commanded to do so. We are to love God with all our being. We are then commanded to love others.

Joyful: Joy is choosing to delight and rejoice in the things of God.

Peaceful: When we think of peace, we may think of the opposite of war. That is not what this peace is all about. Peace is being right with God and knowing that we are in agreement with Him in our lives. It comes from knowing that we are safe from anything that removes our faith in God or our trust in His Word.

Longsuffering: Longsuffering is exhibited in two ways. First, it is the ability to endure trials in our lives and, second, then to endure people. The first builds our ability to accomplish the second.

Gentleness: The best way to define gentleness is this: being useful. A gentle man is one who is pliable and easily used because of a nature that cares for the needs of others. He is able to work with others because he gets along with them.

Goodness: This is a quality that does not take advantage of others, but does what is in the best interest of others. It is kindness with integrity. What we do, we do in the best interest of others, not merely to promote our agenda.

Faith: Without faith it is impossible for us to please God (Hebrews 11:6). Faith is doing what we do because we trust Him. It means we lean on His power and wisdom and not our own.

151

Meekness: This is the opposite of pride. It is the ability to do God's work without becoming entitled or impressed with ourselves. Meekness is looking up to no man, nor down to no man. To be meek is to be on a level plain with others.

Temperance: This is often said to mean that we have good self-control, but it goes further than that. It means that we have control of our strengths. It is the father gently showing discipline to his small child. The father's strength could bring harm, but he has it under control.

Part Four: The Role of a Man

The man with the right purpose and the right character will have the right fruit, and that will lead him to find his role within the "team" or body of the church. Here is the culmination of the process of real manhood. We become team ministers. We find that we have a specific role for which we were created. We are not all made the same, nor were we ever made to be the same. We are all made to perform our own unique role for the work of God, and we are to do it with a love that edifies the body or church.

Let me once again insert Sam and others like him into the conversation. Throughout history, eunuchs have played a unique and wonderful role within the work of God. In the early church, they were valued for their contributions. Their manhood was not in question merely because they were different than others. In fact, they were not considered to be less of a man than others merely because they did not engage in sexual practices. In time, that changed. Tragically, the things that changed society's view of manhood also affected the views of Christians.

What about the "macho" type of men we see in the Bible? What are we to think of men like David who slew Goliath or like Samson a powerful warrior? The Bible is filled with stories of great warriors or men who were wild or rugged. The best way to explain this is to say that they too were ***"born that way."*** God needed them to fill a role the same way he needed those who were born like Sam. We must go back to the fact that God has made each of us to be unique and for His own purpose.

Rugged men are men made for His purpose. More genteel men are men made for His purpose. Men who desire women are men made for His purpose. Men without desires for women are made for His purpose. We tragically define men in the way Satan would have us define them, instead of the way God described them. True biblical manhood ultimately rests in our submission to our Lord and Savior, Jesus Christ. Are we willing to humble ourselves and worship our Creator, and are we willing to recognize Him for whom and what He is?

Chapter Eighteen

THE PRODIGAL EUNUCH

Imagine if the younger son in the famous story Jesus told of the Prodigal Son (Luke 15) was actually a eunuch, and he was confused about his sexual identity. Imagine that, after years of struggling and wondering why he was different, one day he finally knew he had to make a decision. As much as he loved his father, his confusion had tormented him for so long that he knew he had to leave. He felt that in the "gay" far country he could find himself and not disgrace his father, so he made the decision to leave.

He gathered his belongings and left for a world he knew nothing about, but in hopes of finding himself. When he arrived, he was readily accepted by those who felt like him and had also made the same journey. He lived the way they lived, and did things he never dreamed he would do. As guilty as he felt, he at least felt like he belonged. But, deep in his heart, he knew their acceptance was limited and came with conditions. He knew that the true love he longed for was missing. One day, something amazing took place. While sitting in the pig pen of his own sinful choices, he came to himself.

That is the story I have seen dozens of times since I first met Sam. In fact, I have been there many times when a young man or woman finally came to themselves and confessed that they were not "gay," but that they were a eunuch. Can you imagine how freeing, yet how difficult that moment would be? I think of one young man who had lived in the "gay" far country for four years and who had been in a relationship with another man for over a year. Home looked so far away for him. He was not certain how his parents and others would react. He knew that on some level he was accepted where he was, but he had come to himself before he knew he had to try and return home. So, with great fear and uncertainty, he returned home in hopes of being accepted, even if only as a servant. In tears he said, "God forgive me for blaming You for not giving me an answer when the answer was there all along."

This is where the story turns to those of us at home. Unless you understand the difficulty of the return, you may not respond in the proper way, causing the prodigal eunuch to feel they have no place to go but back to the "gay" far country. That ought not to be the case. We must know how to receive them, yet how is a parent to know what they should or should not do? The way we can know is to study what the father did in this timeless story. There are some very important elements in receiving the prodigal eunuch back home.

1. Do not make them feel that they can never come home. No matter how far into the lifestyle they have gone, never believe they have gone too far to come home. The prodigal in the biblical account had gone as far into the depths as it was possible to go, yet his father accepted him home.

2. Lovingly and eagerly accept them back. Do not be suspicious of their motives or of their sincerity. Do not withhold your love for fear they may fall back again. They may struggle, but make certain they feel your acceptance. Remember, they have left the acceptance of the "gay" far country and now they need your acceptance more than ever.

3. Celebrate their return gladly and openly. Yes, show no shame, only joy. Do not hide their return from your church family and do not apologize for accepting them back. Their return should be as joyful as the day they were born into your family.

4. Forget yourself for them. The father ran to greet his son, which meant that his legs were exposed as he did so. That was a shameful thing for a Jewish male to do, but he did not care. His son had come home. It was about his son. This is the hardest thing for some parents to do. They worry about what others are thinking. Forget your pride, and do not even consider yourself. Make the return about your child, not yourself.

5. Do not put conditions on the returning prodigal. The father did not say, "You can return *if...*" In fact, the son attempted to put conditions on

156

himself. In his rehearsed speech, he said, "Make me as one of thy hired servants," but the father never even gave his son the chance to utter those words. The father was just happy his son was home, accepting him with no conditions whatsoever. That is how we should accept the returning prodigal eunuch—unconditionally.

6. Don't ask, but let them tell you what sins they committed if and when they feel they need to. There is no evidence that the Prodigal Son ever told his father what sins he committed in the far country. This is so important. There are things you may wish not to know, but if you have a prodigal eunuch that feels the need to tell you, be prepared not to react. Don't be shocked, incensed, or angry. Just listen with compassion and imagine the pain in that prodigal. However, never feel you must know. Sometimes, they may feel that they do not want to ever share what they did, and you should accept their wishes.

7. Protect them from the elder brothers whom are not happy with the prodigal's return. Yes, there will be some who resent a prodigal eunuch's return home. They could be family members, church members, preachers, and maybe even your own pastor. Do not allow them to run off the prodigal eunuch; be their advocate just as the father advocated to the elder brother in the biblical account. Here are a few ways to protect your prodigal:

- Defend them from accusation. Some will say accusatory things that they know nothing about. Be prepared to deflect these accusations.
- Defend them from accosting. Some will preach at them if given the chance. Don't give them the chance.
- Defend them from accountability. Some will place unreasonable demands on the prodigal eunuch, even more than they would of other returning prodigals. That is wrong. Do not allow it to happen. Be the one who stands between your prodigal and those who want to block their journey back home with silly demands.
- Defend them from accordance. There will be those who will attempt to "normalize" your prodigal eunuch in an attempt to make them conform to their idea of what they should be. They

157

will play matchmaker and try to help them find a good spouse. They will not accept the truth of eunuchism and will do their best to make your prodigal eunuch fit into the status quo mold. Some will never accept them for how God made them. Protect your prodigal from these people.

8. Believe in their sincerity. Notice the very last part of the biblical story. The father said, *"This thy brother was dead, and is alive again; and was lost, and is found."* The father was not saying, "Let's give him a chance to see if he is sincere or if he stays at home." No, he was definitive in his confidence that his son was alive and found. Do not doubt your returning prodigal eunuch. They need to know that you truly believe they are honest and sincere. Have faith that they are home for good. There may be some struggles, but now they will struggle at home. Never again do they need to leave home in confusion. They are home, and you must believe in them.

Parent, brother, sister, grandparent, or other loved one who has a prodigal returning from the "gay" far country, let me ask you a question. Are you spiritual enough to receive and restore that prodigal eunuch? I do not mean restore them to what you once thought they should be, but to restore them to what God made them to be. That is an important question. Are you spiritual enough to support their return and to help them become the eunuch God made them to be? My prayer is that you will do what that father did when his son came home.

Chapter Nineteen
BORN AGAIN EUNUCHS

Sam was born a eunuch. That was always God's purpose for his life. As a young boy, Sam accepted Christ as his Savior. Later, Sam would become confused by his sexual identity and briefly enter into a homosexual lifestyle. Sam was still saved and on his way to Heaven. When Sam recognized his purpose, he left that lifestyle and gave his life to Christ.

It does not matter who you are or what you have done, the most important decision you will ever make is to trust the finished work of Christ for your Salvation. Perhaps you are a eunuch and did not realize it. Perhaps God wants you to understand the life and purpose of a eunuch. However, knowing you are a eunuch, but not having Christ will do you no good in the grand scope of things. You must be born again, a new creature in Christ. Regardless of whom you are, where you have been, or what you have done, God has a specific plan for you.

The Ethiopian Eunuch

It was no coincidence that the first Gentile conversion recorded in the Bible was a eunuch (Acts 8:26-40). The eunuch's name is unknown, but we call him the Ethiopian eunuch. The Ethiopian eunuch, a Gentile, had been visiting the Temple in Jerusalem to worship. He was reading a copy of the book of Isaiah, probably his own copy. The Evangelist Philip was directed to this man by an "angel of the Lord" to go over and join the eunuch's chariot. Phillip had to wonder about this, because this eunuch was of a different race and ethnicity. For these reasons and the fact he was a eunuch, he was considered an outcast and not fully welcomed in the worship community. However, something was special about this man. He was a man of faith, and God honored that. The Holy Spirit could have chosen anyone to be the first Gentile convert, but the Holy Spirit chose a black, Ethiopian eunuch.

The Scripture the eunuch was reading is interesting, because the Prophet Isaiah penned a beautiful passage a few chapters later about a day that would come when all godly eunuchs would be blessed by God in a special way. In Isaiah 56:4-5 it says, *"For thus says the LORD: To the eunuchs who keep my Sabbaths, who choose the things that please me and hold fast my covenant, I will give, in my house and within my walls, a monument and a name better than sons and daughters; I will give them an everlasting name that shall not be cut off."*

The eunuch was reading in Isaiah 53, which says, *"All we like sheep have gone astray; we have turned everyone to his own way; and the Lord hath laid on him the iniquity of us all. He was oppressed, and he was afflicted, yet he opened not his mouth: he is brought as a lamb to the slaughter, and as a sheep before her shearers is dumb, so he openeth not his mouth. He was taken from prison and from judgment: and who shall declare his generation? For he was cut off out of the land of the living: for the transgression of my people was he stricken."*

The term 'cut off' refers to the law that restricted Temple rights to anyone that did not reproduce. The Ethiopian eunuch was reading prophesy concerning a Messiah with whom he could identify. When Phillip asked him if he understood what he was reading, the Ethiopian eunuch said, *"How can I, except some man should guide me"* (Acts 8:31). He then begged Phillip to share with him what he knew. He said, *"I pray you, of whom does the prophet speak? of himself, or of some other man?"* The Scripture says that Phillip *"preached unto him Jesus."*

After the Ethiopian eunuch received the truth, he said, *"I believe that Jesus Christ is the Son of God."* Phillip then baptized this born again eunuch. At last, it all made sense to him. Can you imagine how happy he was? The eunuch, who had always been an outcast of the Temple now understood that his body was the Temple (1 Corinthians 6:15-20).

Do you realize that God chose a eunuch as the first recorded Gentile convert? Can you think of any reason that He might make this choice? Here are a few possibilities:

160

God loves everybody. He was telling us once again that *"whosoever shall call upon the name of the Lord, shall be saved"* (Romans 10:13). "Whosoever" means anybody. Men, women, boys, girls, the blind, the deaf, the disabled, the Jew and the Gentile can all be redeemed. Each can be found in that inclusive word, "whosoever." The Ethiopian eunuch is a wonderful example of salvation. It shows us that God loves us so much that He gave His Only begotten Son who died and rose again to pay the sin debt for all mankind (John 3:16).

God always has a plan and a purpose. How did this eunuch from the deepest part of Africa come to know the Old Testament Scriptures? Judaism had been a presence in Ethiopia for many years. We are told that this Ethiopian was in charge of the whole treasury of the Queen. This was a man with immense power and stature in the nation of Ethiopia.

Legend has it that he went back home and started a church, referred to as "the Eunuch Church." For the last two thousand years, there is only one place that has continually kept its Christian influence, Ethiopia. The Eunuch Church is still alive and well. The Ethiopian eunuch's testimony for Christ is still producing fruit for God's Kingdom. *"Neither let the eunuch say, Behold, I am a dry tree"* (Isaiah 56:3).

God remembers those who honor Him. In 1 Kings 10, we are told about the Queen of Sheba (Ethiopia) traveling to Jerusalem to meet King Solomon where she asked him many difficult questions. The Bible says she was astonished at Solomon's wisdom and began to glorify God. She said, "Blessed be the Lord," and gave Solomon many gifts to be used for God's Temple. In fact, the pillars to the Temple were given by her. One thousand years later, Jesus honors this woman's faith while preaching (Matthew 12:42).

God gives us a glimpse of Glory. If you are a Christian, guess what? You are a future eunuch. Even if you weren't born that way on earth, if you are saved, then you were born again that way. Let me explain; in Matthew 22:30, Jesus says, *"For in the resurrection they neither marry, nor are given in marriage, but are as the angels of God in heaven."* What an awesome truth for all born eunuchs. You, the eunuch, may be the one called different down here, but in Heaven we'll all be eunuchs. In Heaven, there will be no marriages. We'll still be men and women, only we will be *perfected* men and women. We will be like the angels. I wonder if this is why Jesus said His Kingdom was like a bunch of little children, everyone abiding together as one happy family—a family of eunuchs.

Chapter Twenty

REDEEMED EUNUCHS

Sam was already involved in the "gay" lifestyle when all these circumstances took place that brought him back to God. God's grace was greater than the abomination of his sins. This is important, because many feel that once someone has allowed this sin into their life there is no redemption. It is not only Christian brothers and sisters who sometimes feel this way; Satan often deceives the one in the sin to believe it as well. It is a lie. No matter what has transpired in your life, God loves you and has called you for His purpose. *"For the gifts and calling of God are without repentance"* (Romans 11:29). Your fall does not negate His call.

Satan is the deceiver. He cares for no one, but I am convinced that those who are vulnerable to sexual sins are especially in his scope. He knows that, once addicted, they will struggle to ever gain victory in their lives without the power of God. Eunuchs are also under a tremendous attack by Satan. If he can get them to believe they are "homosexual" and lead them into that lifestyle, the effects are immense, not only on them, but on many others.

While not every natural eunuch enters into an unnatural lifestyle, our society heavily influences their thought process in that direction. This influence grows stronger every passing day as the lifestyle becomes more acceptable. Unfortunately, I meet many individuals who discover the truth after they have already been deceived and are ensnared by the sins of the homosexual lifestyle. Once a person has realized they are a born eunuch, they are left with an important decision. Imagine if the life you choose was taken away from you. Suddenly, you are left to make drastic changes from the life that you have known. That is exactly what happens to a man or woman after they have come to the truth regarding these matters.

There is hope for anyone who desires to be freed from the bondage of sin. Christ has already made us free, but we must accept and take the steps necessary to live in that freedom. The steps I prescribe come from two passages of Scripture, both of which are familiar to anyone who has been in church for any length of time: 1 John 1:9 and Romans 12. If you are stepping out of the sexual bondage of homosexuality, please take these principles deeply to heart. You *can* be made free and you *can* have victory if you will trust the Lord and follow His Word. Here are eight steps to freedom.

STEP ONE

There must be a confession of sin. I wish that we could reach every person before they fall into the trap of sexual sin. There are few sins that have a longer or more devastating effect on people than sexual sins. Unfortunately for many, they have already been drawn into the sins of homosexuality before they realize who and what God made them to be. So, what is a eunuch to do if he has already gone down that road?

1 John 1:9 – *If we confess our sins, he is faithful and just to forgive us our sins, and to cleanse us from all unrighteousness.*

Do not despair. God is faithful. In 1 John 1:9, we learn of His faithfulness. What this means to you is that His faithfulness exceeds your sinfulness.

Confession guarantees your forgiveness because He is faithful. Now here is the part that you must understand. God stands ready to forgive, but you must be honest with Him. What you have done is a sin. Ignorance is no excuse. The fact that you were "born that way" cannot exclude you from responsibility. Confess your sin *as sin* honestly before God. Remember, He is faithful to forgive.

God is just. I love this truth because it is His justice that is so vital for our opportunity to be forgiven. His justice means that He is not prejudiced. It means He will not judge you differently than He does others. It means that His justice is the same for all. Most importantly, it means that He is not merely sweeping sin under the rug. He has dealt with it and seen to it that it cannot come up later and be used against us.

164

STEP TWO

There must be a cleansing from unrighteousness. This is crucial to the one who is turning from sexual sin. All sin leaves its own residue, but sexual sins have a much more resilient effect on the sinner. This can only be conquered through a thorough *cleansing* and that cleansing can only come through a thorough *confessing.*

Often, sexual sins are more difficult to admit. For some reason, we feel a stronger sense of guilt and shame over these sins. We come to God and generalize the sins because we are embarrassed to speak of them openly and honestly to God. As a result, the residue is still there, and we struggle for a long time.

When coming out of sexual sin, it is vital for one to have absolute repentance, not merely for each act of sin, but also for each thought and desire. When we have complete and honest repentance with God, it is not merely a release or relief, it is a cleansing. That cleansing is deeper than we could administer ourselves. Christ can clean the hidden parts in us that we cannot reach. This, however, only comes when we come clean with God in total confession, holding nothing back.

STEP THREE

There must be a commitment to chastity. No matter how much God has forgiven you and cleansed you, the next step is critical. You must make a commitment to chastity or, as one man called it, "Christ centered celibacy."

Romans 12:1 – *I beseech you therefore, brethren, by the mercies of God, that ye present your bodies a living sacrifice, holy, acceptable unto God, which is your reasonable service.*

We are told to present our bodies to God as a living sacrifice, and we are to be holy and acceptable. That means we are to set our bodies apart for Him. That is a commitment to live a life of total sexual purity (Romans 12:1). In fact, Romans 12 could be the redemption of Romans 1. There are several descriptions given concerning this commitment to purity.

It is a bodily commitment. So many people undervalue their bodies, but God does not. We are told that our bodies are sacred. Our bodies are the Temple (dwelling place) of the Holy Spirit of God. When you commit sexual sin, you sin against the body, which means you desecrate the Temple of Almighty God. Our Catholic friends have owned a term that needs to be adopted by all eunuchs—celibacy. Eunuchs are to be celibate, which means they must refrain from *all* sexual relationships.

It is a living commitment. Eunuchs must be vigilant every minute of every day, always committed and aware of temptations. You are not dead; you are alive. Therefore, you can never assume that you cannot sin as long as you live. Yes, you are dead to sin, but you are alive in Christ. Only by living for Him can you die to self. Your body is now a vehicle for the work of God. Your commitment to chastity requires that you recognize it is your responsibility, with Christ's help, to care for the body and keep it spiritually fine-tuned. Christ will never ask you to do something impossible. You can do all things through Christ as He strengthens you (Philippians 4:13).

It is a holy commitment. The word "holy" means to be set apart. Let me illustrate. Many years ago, I heard of a church that bought a building that had previously housed a tavern. They bought the building so that it could be used to preach and teach the Word of God. The alcohol and all remnants of the sinful ways that building had been used in the past were removed. It was now set apart for a new purpose. That is what we do when we present our bodies to the Lord as holy. All other sinful uses of the past are removed and our body is set apart to be used only for Him.

It is an acceptable commitment. Celibacy is not merely an extension of the word "holy," but goes even further. What we consider holiness is limited by our sinful natures. What God considers holy is far different. It is not enough that our holiness satisfies the minds of men, but that it satisfies the heart and holiness of God. This means that, when our bodies are acceptable, you must do more than be celibate; we must be sacred, which includes even our thoughts on such things as pornography, masturbation, or other sexual stimuli. *Any* action, internal or external, that desecrates the body is unacceptable to God.

166

All of these are part of us giving our bodies over to the Lord, and if we do so, we can have victory over the sins which overtake us.

STEP FOUR

There must be a case for transformation. Transformation is the opposite of conformation. Conformation is what you become when you try to be like others. Transformation is what you become when you submit yourself to the control of another. How is this accomplished? You need to totally change the way you think. A person who has a sexual "addiction" has a mental problem. The mind keeps replaying the acts of your past, and that causes you to entertain the potential of committing the sin again. You can try to conform to the Christian world and to your church, but it will not work, because you are merely being conformed. A conformer continues to conform to that which is around them. That means that when your environment changes, your behavior changes.

Transformation is the work within you performed by God. This transformation changes you from the inside out. Interestingly, it says in our passage to "be not" and then to "be" (Romans 12:2). It begins with "be not conformed to this world." What does that mean? It means that you cannot merely use the world's methods for changing your life. You cannot get victory with weapons or tools of the flesh. Your weapons are not carnal, but spiritual.

2 Corinthians 10:3-6 – *For though we walk in the flesh, we do not war after the flesh: (For the weapons of our warfare are not carnal, but mighty through God to the pulling down of strong holds;) Casting down imaginations, and every high thing that exalteth itself against the knowledge of God, and bringing into captivity every thought to the obedience of Christ; And having in a readiness to revenge all disobedience, when your obedience is fulfilled.*

The only way strongholds can be pulled down is through spiritual means. We are commanded to "be ye transformed." This is our choice to adopt the spiritual weapons of warfare. God can transform you from within, *if* you use His weapons and not yours. What are His weapons?

Ephesians 6:13-17 – *Wherefore take unto you the whole armour of God, that ye may be able to withstand in the evil day, and having done all, to stand. Stand therefore, having your loins girt about with truth, and having on the breastplate of righteousness; And your feet shod with the preparation of the gospel of peace; Above all, taking the shield of faith, wherewith ye shall be able to quench all the fiery darts of the wicked. And take the helmet of salvation, and the sword of the Spirit, which is the word of God.*

The things that God uses to bring about transformation are truth, righteousness, the gospel of peace, faith, and salvation. The eunuch must put on this "armor of God" if they are to have the victory that comes from transformation.

STEP FIVE

There must be clarity of purpose. Many people fall back into sin because, even after they present their bodies, they miss the purpose of doing so, which is to prove God's will. What does that mean? When a person is born a eunuch, he is born with a special purpose. When he presents his body and God transforms him, his purpose is proven to those around him. The proof of God's purpose does not come first. It comes last.

Romans 12:2b – *That ye may prove what is that good, and acceptable, and perfect, will of God.*

God made you the way you are. Now you must prove His purpose with your life. There are three elements in the will of God for all of us:

His good will is what He made us to be.

His acceptable will is what He made us to do.

His perfect will is what He does through us.

If you are a eunuch, prove what is good. You were born that way to do a work for God, so bring that work to Him to be accepted. He can use that work to accomplish eternal things that are perfected in Him.

STEP SIX

There must be a continuation of humility. It would be easy for a eunuch to be proud of their celibacy and wear it as a badge honoring themselves, rather than Christ. In doing this, they elevate themselves above others. Be careful that you remain humble in your special calling.

Romans 12:3 – *For I say, through the grace given unto me, to every man that is among you, not to think of himself more highly than he ought to think; but to think soberly, according as God hath dealt to every man the measure of faith.*

Nothing is more disappointing than a Christian that is set apart for God, but then becomes self-righteous and acts as though they are better than others. Being a eunuch is a special calling, but it does not make you better than those who are not eunuchs. Jesus made it clear that marriage was a good option for those who are unable to be or to do what you are or do. Peter was not less of a faithful disciple than John, he was merely different. He chose marriage while John did not. John chose chastity while unmarried, and Peter chose chastity in marriage.

STEP SEVEN

There must be cause for service. Eunuchs have special gifts that can be uniquely used within the ministry of a church. They are great servants and have a unique sensitivity to people as well as to the things of God. Let your gifts be used within the family of your church for the glory of God and edification of the church.

Romans 12:5-6 – *For as we have many members in one body, and all members have not the same office: So we, being many, are one body in Christ, and every one members one of another. Having then gifts differing according to the grace that is given to us.*

All of us are a part of the body of believers where God has placed us. Each of us is given a different purpose within that body. The purpose of presenting our bodies is to find and fulfill our purpose, without being jealous or judging others.

STEP EIGHT

There must be a community of believers.

Romans 12:9-10 – *Let love be without dissimulation. Abhor that which is evil; cleave to that which is good. Be kindly affectioned one to another with brotherly love; in honour preferring one another.*

In the work of a church, we must be as one, even though we are all different in personality and in purpose. The eunuch must fit in and be a good testimony. There are a couple of elements I want to warn you about.

Love purely and honestly. Do not pretend you are not what God made you to be and do not live a double life. Live your life honestly before all men.

Abhor evil actions and appearances. When people know your calling and your past, they will watch you. Two eunuchs of the same sex must be careful in the behavior with one another, both publicly and privately. Avoid the appearances of evil.

Draw tight to the good. What is good? Jesus made it clear when He said this about Mary: *"But one thing is needful: and Mary hath chosen that good part, which shall not be taken away from her"* (Luke 10:42). Make sure that you seek your intimacy from the Lord as did Mary and the beloved Apostle John. Please accept this in intended context; Jesus is to be your first love and only lover.

Have the right relationship with your fellow eunuchs. "*Be kindly affectioned one to another with brotherly love"* (Romans 12:10a).

Be unselfish (preferring one another).

I could go on in this passage and show the behavior of one who has sanctified their body. Every one of the items in the list below describes the one whose body has been given over to the Lord. I especially see application in every one of these to those who are eunuchs.

- Not slothful in business
- Fervent in spirit

- Serving the Lord
- Rejoicing in hope
- Patient in tribulation
- Continuing instant in prayer
- Distributing to the necessity of saints
- Given to hospitality
- Bless them which persecute you: bless, and curse not
- Rejoice with them that do rejoice, and weep with them that weep
- Be of the same mind one toward another
- Mind not high things, but condescend to men of low estate
- Be not wise in your own conceits
- Recompense to no man evil for evil
- Provide things honest in the sight of all men
- If it be possible, as much as lieth in you, live peaceably with all men
- Dearly beloved, avenge not yourselves, but rather give place unto wrath: for it is written, vengeance is mine; I will repay, saith the Lord
- Therefore if thine enemy hunger, feed him; if he thirst, give him drink: for in so doing thou shalt heap coals of fire on his head
- Be not overcome of evil, but overcome evil with good

So, that is what a eunuch is to do. You can go from the lifestyle where you came from and one day be totally free and living in great victory. The decision is yours. Begin the journey now. Find the purpose for which you were born and bring glory to the One who made you this way.

Chapter Twenty One

HONORABLE HERITAGE
OF EUNUCHISM

In the office that night, Sam proudly proclaimed, "I am a eunuch." Since that time, I have discovered that the joyous initial discovery of the truth is often followed with a feeling of embarrassment. After all, being a eunuch is not something we *seek* to be. That, plus the fact that many people have a negative reaction to the idea of one being a eunuch often turns their excitement into shame.

"I have a goodly heritage."

The statement above is a quote from the sixteenth Psalm, written by David. Interestingly, the entire Psalm is a fitting prayer or song for anyone, but specifically for one who was born a eunuch.

A heritage is something that we all value. It is what someone has left for us in the way of exemplary behavior in an area which we are living. For example, you will hear athletes speaking of the heritage of their sport, referring to those who went before and led the way for them. We speak of our military heritage and of those who bravely served our country before us. We speak of our Christian heritage, referring to those who paid a price in contending for the faith we now enjoy. Heritages are comforting, encouraging, inspiring and enlightening. We all seek to know our heritage.

My eunuch friend, you have a heritage!

There has been much written throughout history about eunuchs, and history distinguishes between the different types. There is a heritage of eunuchs who were born as eunuchs. In meeting with eunuchs, I have discovered that it is quite comforting for them to learn that this is not something new, although it has been ignored and even scorned for a long time. There is a term used in this book that is a great summation of Matthew 19 eunuchism and that term is "Faithfully Unmarried." Throughout history, you will find a plethora of individuals of whom we could easily identify as Faithfully Unmarried.

Some of the most renowned Bible commentary writers in history have had great insight concerning the born-eunuch.

In Ecclesiastes 1:9, King Solomon said, "There is no new thing under the sun." The information provided in this book concerning the teaching on eunuchs is nothing new. Many men from the past have written and preached on this topic. In this chapter, we provide a few examples with comments and excerpts from their writings. We begin with comments from the third century by Origen, and we end with an excerpt from a sermon given by John Wesley (The Father of Methodism).

Historical Theologians' Comments on Matthew 19:11-12

Disclaimer: The quotes from the men below are not a declaration of our personal agreement with their doctrinal positions, but rather as proof that the subject of eunuchism is not a new idea or teaching.

Origen Adamantius (184/185 – 253/254, Scholar, Christian theologian and Church Father)

Among those who live abstinently in this regard, however, there are, in my opinion, three different groups. The first are so because of their nature*; to them the word should be applicable: There are eunuchs who are born so from their mother's womb. But it is a great power to grasp the eunuchization of the soul through the Word, which not all can grasp, but only they to whom it is given. But it is given to all those who ask God for the rational sword and*

174

who use it as appropriate to eunuchize themselves for the kingdom of heaven's sake...

But one must know that no small number of arguments to prove that the three eunuchizations are to be understood physically will be found by anyone who would like to prove that and would agree with those who have been mentioned before who teach this in their writings. But we did not want to present these arguments in order not to provide an occasion - simply by presenting these sayings as an exercise and offering a solution for each - for those, who do not grasp the saying on eunuchism the way Jesus intends it, to understand the word "grasp" in a different meaning than is necessary, i.e, to understand it physically, even though it is necessary that one who lives and moves in the spirit [Galatians 5:25] should be convinced that the three eunuchizations are also meant spiritually.

Jerome (Saint Jerome, *Latin: Eusebius* 347 – 420, a Latin Christian priest, confessor, theologian and historian, who also became a Doctor of the Church.)

Letter 22, To Eustochius: The eunuchs from their mother's womb are those who have a frigid nature and have no appetite for (female) lust, and those who are made by people are either those who are made by philosophers or those who are softened into women for the sake of the cult of idols, or who simulate chastity due to heretical persuasion so as to fake the truth of religion.

"Whoever can grasp this, let him grasp it," so that every single one will consider his strength as to whether he can fulfill virginity and the rules of purity. For chastity is pleasant per se, and attractive to anyone. But one's strength has to be considered so that let him who is able to grasp this, let him grasp it. The voice of the Lord is, so to speak, encouraging and exciting his soldiers toward the reward of purity: Whoever can grasp this, let him grasp it, whoever can fight, let him fight, conquer, and triumph.

Augustine of Hippo (Saint Augustine, 354 – 430, Early Christian theologian whose writings are considered very influential in the development of Western Christianity and Western philosophy).

Let us hear the Lord Himself delivering most plain judgment on this matter. For, upon His speaking after a divine and fearful manner concerning husband and wife not separating, save on account of fornication, His disciples said to Him, "If the case be such with a wife, it is not good to marry." To whom He saith, "Not all receive this saying. For there are eunuchs who were so born: What could be said more true, what more clear?

Therefore go on, Saints of God, boys and girls, males and females, unmarried men, and women; go on and persevere unto the end. Praise more sweetly the Lord, Whom ye think on more richly: hope more happily in Him, Whom ye serve more instantly: love more ardently Him, whom ye please more attentively. With loins girded, and lamps burning, wait for the Lord, when He cometh from the marriage. Ye shall bring unto the marriage of the Lamb a new song, which ye shall sing on your harps. Not surely such as the whole earth singeth, unto which it is said, "Sing unto the Lord a new song; sing unto the Lord, the whole earth" : but such as no one shall be able to utter but you.

Joy of the virgins of Christ, in Christ, with Christ, after Christ, through Christ, for Christ. The joys peculiar to the virgins of Christ, are not the same as of such as are not virgins, although of Christ. For there are to different persons different joys, but to none such. Go (enter) into these, follow the Lamb, because the Flesh of the Lamb also is assuredly virgin. For this He retained in Himself when grown up, which He took not away from His Mother by His conception and birth. Follow Him, as ye deserve, in virginity of heart and flesh, wheresoever He shall have gone. For what is it to follow, but to imitate?

(Women) If, therefore, ye despise marriages of sons of men, from which to beget sons of men, love ye with your whole heart Him,

176

Who is fair of form above the sons of men; ye have leisure; your heart is free from marriage bonds. Gaze on the Beauty of your Lover: think of Him equal to the Father, made subject also to His mother: ruling even in the heavens, and serving upon the earth: creating all things, created among all things. That very thing, which in Him the proud mock at, gaze on, how fair it is: with inward eyes gaze on the wounds of Him hanging, the scars of Him rising again, the blood of Him dying, the price of him that believes, the gain of Him that redeems. Consider of how great value these are, weigh them in the scales of Charity; and whatever of love ye had to expend upon your marriages, pay back to Him. It is well that He seeks your beauty within, where He hath given unto you power to become daughters of God: He seeks not of you a fair flesh, but fair conduct.

John Calvin (a 16th century religious leader)

The gift of born celibacy is a special gift; for when Christ says that all are not capable of receiving it, but those to whom it is given, he plainly shows that it was not given to all. And this reproves the pride of those who do not hesitate to claim for themselves what Christ so manifestly refuses to them.

Charles Spurgeon (great 19th century pastor)

Some have but feeble desires concerning marriage (relations) and they were so born. They will find it good to remain as they are. Violations of purity are abominable in the sight of the Lord.

Matthew Henry (Bible Commentary)

He (God) allows it good for some not to marry; "He that is able to receive it, let him receive it." Christ allowed what the disciples said, It is good not to marry; not as an objection against the prohibition of divorce, as they intended it, but as giving them a rule (perhaps no less unpleasing to them), that they who have the gift of continence, and are not under any necessity of marrying, do best if they continue single (1 Co. 7:1); for they that are

177

unmarried have opportunity, if they have but a heart, to care more "for the things of the Lord, how they may please the Lord" (1 Co. 7:32-34). Being less encumbered with the cares of this life, and having a greater vacancy of thought and time to mind better things. The increase of grace is better than the increase of the family, and fellowship with the Father and with his Son Jesus Christ is to be preferred before any other fellowship.

McGarvey and Pendleton (Bible Commentary)

My understanding of the passage is this: The disciples, startled by the Lord's declaration as to the indissolubility of marriage, declared that marriage was inexpedient. Jesus accepts their saying, because applicable to but three cases. Jesus is therefore speaking with regard to "celibacy" and "divorce". He says that eunuchs are unfit for marriage, whether made so by nature or by the violence of man. The two first--the "physical" eunuch--are introduced to illustrate the last or "spiritual" eunuch--the man whose intense interest in the affairs of the kingdom of heaven makes him prefer the celibate state. The saying is indeed hard to receive, for it borders on the abnormal and unnatural, and hence it is no command save to those who, being in that abnormal and almost unnatural condition, are in a shape to receive it. Marriage is the natural condition of man, and celibacy is (seemingly) abnormal, but to some extent Biblically countenanced. The trend of Scripture shows that Jesus here speaks about celibacy and not about divorce, for it has much to say about the celibate principle involved here.

John Wesley's Bible Commentary

Verse 11. *But he said to them - This is not universally true; it does not hold, with regard to all men, but with regard to those only to whom is given this excellent gift of God. Now this is given to three sorts of persons to some by natural constitution, without their choice: to others by violence, against their choice; and to others by grace with their choice: who steadily withstand their natural*

inclinations that they may wait upon God without distraction.
Verse 12. *There are eunuchs who have made themselves eunuchs for the kingdom of heaven's sake - Happy they! Who have abstained from marriage (though without condemning or despising it) that they might walk more closely with God! He that is able to receive it, let him receive it - This gracious command (for such it is unquestionably, since to say, such a man may live single, is saying nothing. Who ever doubted this?) is not designed for all men: but only for those few who are able to receive it. O let these receive it joyfully!*

John Wesley (1703 – 1791), Father of Methodism, concerning the eunuch; an excerpt from one of his many insightful sermons:

To this happy few I say know the advantages you enjoy, many of which are pointed out by the apostle himself. You may be without carefulness. You are under no necessity of "caring for the things of the world." You have only to "care for the things of the Lord, how you may please the Lord." One care alone lies upon you, how you "may be holy both in body and spirit."

You may "attend upon the Lord without distraction"; while others, like Martha, are cumbered with much serving and drawn hither and thither by many things, you may remain centered in God, sitting, like Mary, at the Master's feet and listening to every word of his mouth.

You enjoy a blessed liberty from the "trouble in the flesh," which must more or less attend a married state, from a thousand nameless domestic trials which are found sooner or later in every family. You are exempt from numberless occasions of sorrow and anxiety, with which heads of families are entangled; especially those who have sickly, or weak, or unhappy, or disobedient children. If your servants are wicked, you may put them away, and your relation to them ceases. But what could you do with a wicked son or daughter? How could you dissolve that relation?

179

Above all, you are at liberty from the greatest of all entanglements, the loving one creature above all others. It is possible to do this without sin, without any impeachment of our love to God. But how inconceivably difficult to give God our whole heart while a creature has so large a share of it! How much more easily may we do this, when the heart is tenderly, indeed, but equally attached to more than one; or, at least, without any great inequality! What angelic wisdom does it require to give enough of our affection, and not too much, to so near a relation!

And how much easier is it (just to touch on one point more) wholly to conquer our natural desires than to gratify them exactly so far as Christian temperance allows! Just so far as every pleasure of sense prepares us for taking pleasure in God.

You have leisure to improve yourself in every kind, to wait upon God in public and private, and to do good to your neighbor in various ways, as Christian prudence shall suggest; whereas those who are married are necessarily taken up with the things of the world. You may give all your time to God without interruption and need ask leave of none but yourself so to do. You may employ every hour in what you judge to be the most excellent way. But if you were married, you may ask leave of your companion; otherwise what complaints or disgust would follow! And how hard is it even to know (how much more to act suitably to that knowledge) how far you ought to give way, for peace's sake, and where to stop! What wisdom is requisite in order to know how far you can recede from what is most excellent, particularly with regard to conversation that is not "to the use of edifying," in order to please your good-natured or ill-natured partner, without displeasing God!

You may give all your worldly substance to God; nothing need hinder. You have no increasing family; you have no wife or children to provide for which might occasion a thousand doubts whether you had done either too much or too little for them. You may "make yourself friends of" all "the mammon of unrighteousness" which God entrusts you with; having none that has any right to complain, or to charge you with unkindness for so doing. You may lay out all your talents of every kind entirely for the glory of God; as you have none else to please, none to regard but him that lived and died for you.

I say, (dear eunuch) prize the advantages you enjoy; know the value of them. Esteem them as highly while you have them as others do after they have lost them."

Yes, there have been many throughout history who have lived lives as eunuchs though in many cases the word was not always prescribed to them. So why is this important to you? You must know that your calling is special and uniquely designed by God. It is not a fluke nor is it an accident. God in His wisdom has throughout history called a group of men and women to specifically be set aside from marriage in order to do something special for Him. That heritage has been lost or hidden because Satan saw it as a way to prevent many from finding their true calling as well as to disturb the natural order of God. Remember, you can also testify as David did and say "I have a goodly heritage."

Chapter Twenty Two
BELOVED EUNUCHS

I have met and counseled with many young men like Sam who have discovered their calling to be a eunuch. If I had to choose one word to describe these young men, it would have to be "beloved." In fact, I have heard many others speak of eunuchs in similar terms. The word *"beloved"* literally means "loved, esteemed, dear, favorite, and worthy of love." A beloved was one who was comfortable in an intimate relationship with the one who loved them. They were considered beloved because they were favored and enjoyed a special intimacy. Jesus was the beloved Son of the Father, so He enjoyed a favored status with the Father.

When Jesus spoke to the disciples about marriage in Matthew 19, He no doubt had a purpose and knew exactly what He was doing. Perhaps He was suggesting that some of them should consider becoming eunuchs in the faith and was giving them the freedom to choose to be married, even suggesting that one or more of them were born eunuchs and, if so, that it was perfectly normal. I choose to believe that He was doing all three. In fact, He specifically addressed at least one of them with receiving this truth when he said, *"He that is able to receive it, let him receive it."* So, who could that one have been?

As far as we know, all of the disciples were married, except for James and John. Both of these men were young when they were called and, in fact, were still living with their mother. James would be the first apostle who would die a martyr's death. He was still a young man when he died. John, on the other hand, would be the sole apostle who would not die as a martyr, but would outlive all the other apostles. This was, of course, prophesied by the Lord. So, we know that John lived a long life as an unmarried man and, no doubt, a chaste one as well.

The real question is this: Was John the Beloved a "born that way" eunuch? Although we cannot say for sure, it would certainly not be a surprise to me if he was indeed born that way. John definitely was a unique disciple and one who had different qualities than the others. If there was one disciple Jesus was specifically speaking to, then John would be the one. Several times Jesus spoke about a particular person without actually calling him out. He pointed out the fact that Peter was going to deny Him three times and that Judas was going to betray him. While we can look back at these and identify exactly who He was referring to, it is certain that the others did not necessarily know. They could have speculated, but Jesus was a bit vague. Jesus took the opportunity to speak on the subject of eunuchs, and His reason may have been to let John know that he was chosen for a particular purpose and being a eunuch was a part of that purpose.

Premises and Inference

Jesus had three disciples that were closer to Him than all the rest. These three disciples are often referred to as the inner-circle. They were Peter, James, and John. Peter, of course, was married. James and John were sons of a fisherman, James probably being the older of the two. When Jesus called them to follow Him, they left their occupation and began to follow Him. These three "inner-circle" disciples were witnesses to three particular events that the other disciples did not witness, including the transfiguration and Jesus' agony in the Garden of Gethsemane. Neither James nor John appeared to have been married, and their mother was a bold and doting woman as seen in her attempt to ask for special places in Christ's kingdom for her sons. Both of these men were masculine. They had followed in their father's footsteps and taken the occupation of fishermen, which was a rugged way of life. They also were men who were labeled as the "sons of thunder," because of their desire to call down lightning on a village that rejected Christ.

John had some personality traits that I have also seen in many eunuchs, which led me to believe that John may have been the beloved eunuch. Here are some of those traits.

184

John was not afraid of physical intimacy with Jesus. No other disciple was said to have leaned on the breast of Jesus, except John. Sadly, many today equate intimacy with sexuality, but they are two different things entirely. Intimacy is based upon emotional attachment while sexuality is based more upon physical desires. John felt completely comfortable putting his head on Jesus' breast and did not consider it to be strange.

John was tender. Yes, he was known as one of the sons of thunder, but he also was a gentle soul. He often was the antithesis to the Apostle Peter. John was courageous, yet timid. He was the lone disciple at the foot of the Cross, yet he refused to enter the dark open tomb by himself, waiting instead for Peter to go in first.

John described himself as being the disciple that Jesus loved, not once, but four times in his gospel. This term was one that could only be made by a man who felt secure with himself. Something that should be noted here is the fact that there is no apparent jealousy among the other disciples for the title which he gave himself. Perhaps they knew that John was that "one" about whom Jesus was speaking in Matthew 19.

John wrote much on the subject of love in his epistles, and became known as the "apostle of love." All three of his epistles contain much information regarding the subject of loving one another. The gospel of John similarly speaks of love quite frequently. Was it the fact that he was more loving than the other writers that he was inspired by the Holy Spirit to author so many things about love?

John possessed a caring nature. He, like Paul, identified fellow believers as his children. John goes even further in his descriptive penmanship as the only New Testament writer to address a local church body as a "lady" and "sister" whom he loves. The only other apostle to use intimate terms of relation was Paul, whom we know with certainty was a eunuch.

John was the one to whom Jesus looked and said, "Behold thy mother," while hanging on the Cross. Jesus could have assigned that duty to others, including His own half siblings, but perhaps He knew John would never get married, thus allowing him to give better care to Mary.

John was the one who penned prolific and glowing words about eunuchs in Revelation 14:4. There John describes those who are "first fruits" and "not defiled by women," as not only followers of Jesus the "Shepherd," but also as followers of Jesus the "Lamb." He proclaims these Christians as "they which follow the Lamb whithersoever he goeth." Only one disciple followed the Lord, in His earthly ministry, as the Lamb before the slaughter. Only one stood at the foot of the Cross. Only one disciple trusted Christ's resurrection sight unseen. Apparently, John had a special place in his heart towards eunuchs, perhaps because he himself was one.

John was a little temperamental and emotional. This may ruffle a few feathers, but in most cases, women are more emotional and even temperamental. That is the result of the fact that they are more sensitive and nurturing. However, the result can often end up creating some petty jealousies as well as the desire for special attention. From my observations, men born as eunuchs usually exhibit these same characteristics.

In one instance, to which I have already referred, John and his brother were seeking a ball of fire from Heaven to fall on the half-breed Samaritans. Jesus sharply rebuked him and also referred to him and his brother, James, as the "sons of thunder." This term undoubtedly carried a message much like Peter's other name, "Simon." When Jesus rebuked or disciplined Peter, He called him "Simon." John was a "son of thunder," which is not an indication of impetuous anger, but a title of "unproductive commotion." So, we see that John's constitution was one that could easily draw attention for no good reason.

John also desired special treatment from Jesus, even volleying for a better position with Him. This angered the other disciples, but apparently, John did not care. He wanted Jesus to treat him special. Even the name he gave to himself possessed a little bit of elitism. Calling himself "the disciple whom Jesus loved" could have caused others to see him as thinking he had a closer relationship with Jesus.

There are other things that make me wonder if John was not born differently from the other disciples:

- Jesus often placed Peter, the alpha-male, with John the Beloved.
- Jesus chose John as the torch bearer and nurturer of the first established churches.
- Jesus chose John as the Revelator.

John certainly was unique among the disciples, and the fact that he lived a long life without ever being married is in itself a good indicator to the fact that he was a eunuch. We do not know for certain if John chose that life or if he was born that way. What is certain is that there are many men and women who are born as eunuchs and who often deal with great confusion and struggles, *because unlike* Jesus, we do not value them for the special work they can do and for the special people they were born to be.

Chapter Twenty Three
THE ROAD AHEAD

His eyes were filled with tears and his heart with a newfound certainty the evening Sam spoke these words that he was a eunuch and not "gay." Many times since then I have heard similar words spoken by men and women who have discovered their true identity. As this book comes to its conclusion, I trust that it has done two things for you. First, I hope that it has presented the truth by providing important answers to your questions. Secondly, I trust that you have been made free by actually experiencing these truths in your life. If you are one that was "born that way" as a eunuch, I know this has been a journey for you. Let's summarize the road I hope you have taken to the truth.

Your Freedom

The Bible says that if we know the truth it will make us free. Truth is a wonderful thing, yet its wonders are only as good as our reception and response to it. Knowledge of the truth comes in two forms. The first form of this knowledge is intellectual and the second is experiential. If you have knowledge of the truth and do nothing about it, then it only enslaves you further. When we are told in John 8:32 that, if we know the truth, we would be made free, it is speaking of knowing from experience, not merely intellectual knowledge. For example, if you know the speed limit is sixty, but go ninety, you are not free from the consequences of your actions. To know it is sixty and to actually drive sixty is to know the truth that makes you free.

Your Confusion

Many men and women have found themselves mired in confusion because of their lack of attraction towards the opposite sex. It has left them exasperated, wondering why they do not have "normal" feelings. Sadly, much of the confusion was frustrated by the confusing answers given by sincere people who cared about them.

My wife has reminded me through the years that what a man says is often not what a woman hears. In other words, what we say is important, but how we say it is equally or more important. Sam was told many times by friends, family, and his church how much they loved him and that he was always welcome. They were serious about that too, but Sam felt like he was drowning in loneliness. Why? Could it be that love was lost in the translation? As they say in the Army, Sam couldn't quite pick up what they were laying down, maybe because what they were saying did not mesh with how they were saying it. In any case, Sam was confused. The people he loved were confused as well.

Hopefully, much of your confusion has been eliminated from your mind. Now, hopefully, you can see clearly why you are the way you are.

Your Comfort Zone

There is not one among us who does not seek to find a comfort zone in which we can live. We all want to belong. When we feel like we do not belong in one place or in one group, we begin seeking another. Perhaps that is the best explanation for why people that were born to be eunuchs often end up in the "gay" world. It is a place where they feel accepted. It becomes a comfort zone. Satan feasts on doubters and makes them feel welcome even when churches do not.

One of the most useless ways to spend your life is trying to make sense out of nonsense. God is not the author of confusion, yet that period in Sam's life had become a kaleidoscope from which he could see no clear direction. The devil is smart enough to know that God's children will not likely swallow a bold lie; so instead, he gives them a partial truth. Remember, a half truth is a whole lie. Satan loves for those like Sam to know they are different, but he does not want them to know why. I do not believe that Satan is worried much about Christians preaching against unnatural attractions, so long as they do not have clear alternatives.

Now is the time to leave your comfort zone from a life of being comfortable. You can now be at peace with what God made you. Real comfort is not in a zone, it is in a purpose. It is in knowing why you were "born that way." Just like a tree tossed in the road from a storm, no one can move forward until we are willing to unbuckle the seat belt, step out into the rain, and help move the tree. We must get out of our comfort zone in order to live in the truth.

Your Cross

Jesus said, *"If any man will come after me, let him deny himself, and take up his cross daily, and follow me"* (Luke 9:23). Jesus' words imply that there is a cross meant for each individual. Something you need to look at and strongly consider. It is something you can even refuse, but shouldn't. This is why we incorrectly apply this verse a good deal of the time when we say, "Well, that is a cross I will have to bear." For example, I have a good friend who is restricted to a wheelchair. For sure, he would like to be out of it, and it is absolutely a burden in his life. Yet it's plain he did not choose the wheelchair, so his wheelchair is not a version of the cross Jesus was talking about. Many people have burdens in life that were not of their choosing. While providential burdens can be used as a great testimony for the Lord, they are not our personal, individual cross. Sam's cross was not the fact that he was born a eunuch. Sam's cross is Sam's cross, but what exactly is his cross?

When did Jesus (in His humanity) choose his Cross? The Bible tells us about the night Christ was betrayed. Before Judas arrived with the Temple guard, Jesus had been praying. In fact, the Bible says He was praying in agony, "Father, if thou be willing, remove this cup from me" (Luke 22:42). What was His cup? It was the reproach that came with going to the Cross. He was to bear my reproach and your reproach. He had a choice. He said, "Nevertheless." What a powerful word. That's the word that enabled Jesus to take up His cross: "Nevertheless, not my will, but thine, be done."

So what is Sam's cross? It is in bearing the reproach of fulfilling his purpose even as Christ did. Yes, reproach. That is the cross we all must bear. No matter what God calls us to do, we must be willing to bear the reproach. When I was in the military, I had to bear the reproach of not doing what most of the other soldiers were doing. Every cross has a cup of reproach and that includes the cross of the eunuch. Your reproach will be different than mine, but it will be a reproach you must decide to accept in the same way Christ accepted His reproach. The greater the reproach, the more in tune we are with our Savior. The reproach you felt long ago, before you knew the truth, must now be accepted willingly

What is your individual cross? It is the laying down of your wants and desires for the sake of others. How do you do it? It's not easy, but it is simple. Even when your desires and your wants are good, they are still yours. Lay them down. Take up your cross and follow Jesus. How do you lay them down? Do you do it by no longer desiring them? No, this is not the answer. Be honest; it's never fun giving up your wants, and God understands that more than we know. Your decision must be to make a daily declaration, "God, this is what I want; nevertheless, not my will, but Your will be done." Joy comes when our wants line up perfectly with His wants. God's love for the world is what motivated Jesus to take up His cross. Our love for Him and our love for others should motivate us to take up our cross as well.

Your Crown

There is a crown for those who have been called, if they fulfill that call by taking up their cross. The crown for chastity is wonderful, but it becomes a glorious crown when you add celibacy. Fanny Crosby, a famous hymn writer from many years ago, was completely blind. About her blindness, Fanny said, "It seemed intended by the blessed providence of God that I should be blind all my life, and I thank Him for the dispensation. If perfect earthly sight were offered me tomorrow, I would not accept it. I might not have sung hymns to the praise of God if I had been distracted by the beautiful and interesting things about me. If I had a choice, I would still choose to remain blind...for when I die, the first face I will ever see will be the face of my blessed Savior."

What great perspective she had. If you are reading this, perhaps you feel like you can identify with those like Sam. If you were born a eunuch, please know that Heaven will make up for every single moment that you were bullied, made fun of, or were misunderstood. In Heaven there will be no more tears or confusion, and there will be crowns for those who accepted their cup.

Your Christ

Is not this the real issue? When we consider what Christ has done for us, is there any "sacrifice" that we could make that would be too great for Him? When we consider that He never knew what it was to be "normal," why should we be unwilling to be like Him? In His manhood, He never dated. He never intimately knew a woman. He never had a wife or a family. He never had a home of His own. He never felt the embrace of a partner when He arrived home after a weary day of helping people. He never knew what it was like to lay in bed with one He loved. He had no wedding of His own. Jesus gave up all of Heaven to come to earth and be the least "normal" person who ever lived.

Your Choice

No one can make a choice for us as to how we react with the truth we learn. Once it is learned, we are left with the fact that we can never again make excuses. Let's confirm the truth that you are able to be pure before God, no matter how far into sin you have gone. If you were deep into the "homosexual" or "lesbian" lifestyle, you have absolute liberty to return to Christ and be cleansed.

You do not have to live in guilt or shame, because you can be completely forgiven. However, that liberty comes from a single and extremely misunderstood word—repentance. You must repent. Now that does not mean that you must do penance of some kind or crawl on your hands and knees back to God.

Repentance is a change of mind. Let me explain. You decide to take a trip from Atlanta, Georgia, to Chicago, Illinois. You get in your car and begin to drive south on Interstate 75. You are driving along, believing that you are on your way to Chicago, when someone explains to you the truth that I-75 South will take you to Florida, not Chicago. Now you know the truth, but what are you going to do with that truth? Are you going to continue driving, knowing full well that you will not go to Chicago? Or are you going to change your mind and take the route based on the truth you have received? If you change your mind about which direction you are going to take, you have repented.

Likewise, you must now take the truth and repent or change your mind as to the direction you are going to take with your life. The first choice you must make is to become chaste or sexually pure in your life. No more sex outside of the marriage of a husband and wife. That is non-negotiable if you are going to follow Christ.

The next choice is about the life you are going to choose to live. Yes, it is possible that you could totally change your direction and pursue a "normal married life" with the opposite sex, even though you have no desires. Your other choice it to submit to that which God has made you to be, a eunuch. I do not believe God would be displeased with either choice, but which one is going to bring you the greatest earthly satisfaction and eternal rewards?

Your Confession

In everyone's life, we are brought face to face with choices that require a commitment. I take you back to where we began on this journey, that evening when I shared these truths with Sam. That fine young man faced what you face today. He accepted and acted on the truth, sincerely and honestly. Perhaps your words will echo his: *"I am not gay...I am a eunuch."*